How to Shine at Work

How to Shine at Work

Linda R. Dominguez

McGraw-Hill

New York   Chicago   San Francisco
Lisbon   London   Madrid   Mexico City   Milan
New Delhi   San Juan   Seoul   Singapore
Sydney   Toronto

McGraw-Hill

A Division of The **McGraw·Hill** Companies

Copyright ©2003 by McGraw-Hill. All rights reserved. Printed in the United States of America. Except as permitted under the United States Copyright Act of 1976, no part of this publication may be reproduced or distributed in any form or by any means, or stored in a data base or retrieval system, without the prior written permission of the publisher.

1 2 3 4 5 6 7 8 9 0   DOC/DOC   0 9 8 7 6 5 4 3

isbn: 0-07-140865-7

This publication is designed to provide accurate and authoritative information in regard to the subject matter covered. It is sold with the understanding that neither the author nor the publisher is engaged in rendering legal, accounting, or other professional service. If legal advice or other expert assistance is required, the services of a competent professional person should be sought.
> —*From a Declaration of Principles jointly adopted by a Committee of the American Bar Association and a Committee of Publishers*

McGraw-Hill books are available at special quantity discounts to use as premiums and sales promotions, or for use in corporate training programs. For more information, please write to the Director of Special Sales, Professional Publishing, McGraw-Hill, Two Penn Plaza, New York, NY 10121-2298. Or contact your local bookstore.

Library of Congress Cataloging-in-Publication Data

Dominguez, Linda.
   How to shine at work / by Linda Dominguez.
      p.   cm.
   ISBN 0-07-140865-7
   1. Career development. 2. Managing your boss. 3. Interpersonal
   relations. 4. Job satisfaction. I. Title.
   HF5381 .D528
   650.1—dc21

                                        2003007870

This book is printed on recycled, acid-free paper containing a minimum of 50% recycled de-inked fiber.

To my son Josh, his wife Denyse, and their son Gabriel—and to my son Joe, his wife Natascha and their son Anthony. These six people bring joy, love, and balance to my life, allowing me to better develop my vision and honor my values.

To my friend, Gina Dias, who has been a beacon of strength and integrity during my entire adult life, and a constant reminder of how our choices lead us forward, if we let them.

Contents

Preface

When you buy a computer, you get an instruction manual on how to operate it. How would it be to have instructions on how to deal with people, a key component of your campaign to get along in your workplace and your life?

For the longest time, I wished I had two instruction manuals: one with instructions for raising teenagers and one with instructions on building a career I loved as part of a life I loved. Over a period of 25 years, I bounced from one corporate job to another—always making more money, always moving up the proverbial corporate ladder (corner office and all). But the unfulfilling jobs I held were second only to the jobs I hated. As a result, I was not a very nice person to be around. I was not happy, and anyone who knew me knew it.

I had read about personal coaching in the mid-1990s and liked the idea of having "an agent" of sorts guide me to create a life and career I loved. I hired a formally trained, certified coach, and she helped me shine a light on the patterns I had developed and the choices I had made. I came to realize how easy it was to make smarter choices and have professional success and personal fulfillment at the same time.

My coach helped me define myself in terms of values, standards, and boundaries. We looked at who I was, what I wanted, and how I was going to get it. I enrolled in formal coach training with Coach U, strengthened my own personal foundation, and learned new tools and techniques to deal with anything that would come my way—any change, any issue, any difficult person, anything.

I opened my own private coaching practice and now work with healthy professionals and executives who, like me 10 years ago, know that there's more to their career and life than they are currently experiencing and are ready to make some changes.

Coach Thyself

This book is designed for anyone who holds a job in any industry. You will learn the concepts, tips, tools, techniques, and strategies needed to build the success you want—and deserve. The strategies defined in this book, when applied to the areas of getting along and getting ahead in the workplace or moving on to another career, will help you take an objective view of your circumstances, opportunities, barriers, and choices. They will guide you to informed, strategic decisions so that you can take charge of your career and improve your life.

This book does not address typical career counseling subjects. Here you will find exactly what you need today to get along in your workplace, move ahead in your career, increase your income—and, if necessary, learn how to recognize when it's time to move on. You will learn how to navigate through office politics, overcome obstacles, make knowledgeable choices, recognize options, manage change, be accountable, be visible, be credible, take smart risks, move forward, turn any situation around, and have fun doing it.

The What

In today's workplace, what will it take to survive, accomplish, deliver results, succeed, move ahead, lead others, and find satisfaction? With a work environment filled with mergers, acquisitions, reorganizations, downsizing, dot-bombs, and multimillion dollar corporate bankruptcies, career success has been redefined. You will need more than hard work and long hours to get there.

In Part 1 you will learn the process of getting along at work, with clear definitions of career hazard zones and style differences. You will also be given multiple strategies for overcoming the perils of office politics, bully bosses, and cranky coworkers.

Part 2 will help you create a plan for moving ahead in your career, whether you want to improve your reputation, increase your visibility, or get a promotion or salary increase—all by taking control and making smart choices. You will learn how to deal with management-level office politics, how to create visibility without arrogance, how to coach your manager, how to deliver results, how to outshine your coworkers, and how to market yourself into a career that brings you more money and more fun.

Part 3 helps you create a graceful exit plan: When it's time to leave a job, you can go kicking and screaming or you can leave with a great reputation and exit package. But when it's time to go, you're going to go. You will learn how to evaluate your situation and move on and how to orchestrate an exit without guilt and without enemies. This section will also teach you how to manage your job search campaign as a project, with special emphasis on the four routes to landing your new career.

Part 4 will give you a glimpse of what is available to you when you do take control of your career and your life. It will include important concepts to remember as you create your plan for a job you love.

Throughout this book, you will read vivid examples of others who have successfully wrestled with the cycles of harmony and disruption in our work world, including some of my own experiences. You will also have an opportunity to use the worksheets and self-assessments to apply the concepts and strategies to your specific situation.

If you understand that there is a gap between where you are right now and where you want to be and you are willing to take responsibility for your career success and to try something new, then let's get started.

Acknowledgments

I want to acknowledge and thank those who supported me through this process:

My coach, Sandy Vilas, President of CoachU, who helped me get out of my own way, so the words would come.

My friends, colleagues, and clients who relentlessly supported me in my creation of this book: Coach Cynthia Bahnuik, Coach Bridget Copley, clients Philip Topham, Brett Lippel, David Wiberg, Daniel Vickers, and ex-boss and long time friend, Ken Kral, for allowing me to work with them and share their stories.

And to my first coach, Marcia Reynolds, who helped me get started on my journey to escape corporate misery.

PART I

GETTING ALONG

The legend of "The Blind Men and the Elephant," written by John Godfrey Saxe in the late 1800s, told the story of six vision-impaired men, each valuing continuous learning, who wanted to "see" an elephant. The first man, the legend goes, reached out to touch the huge elephant's broad side, and decided that an elephant was like a wall. The second man grasped the animal's tusk, and, feeling that it was round, smooth, and sharp, decided that an elephant was much like a spear. The third man took the elephant's squirming trunk into his hands, and determined that an elephant resembled a snake. The fourth man felt the elephant's sturdy leg, and decided that an elephant seemed a lot like a tree. The fifth grabbed a large, flat ear, and determined that an elephant was like a fan. The sixth grabbed the swinging tail of the animal, and determined that an elephant was just like a rope. And, as the leg-

1

end goes, they each vigorously defended their defined truth, because each was a little bit right, and each was very wrong.

Much of what you will learn in the following chapters will remind you of the six men in this legend. We each have differing frames of reference, diverse senses of urgency, and dissimilar vantage points. For each of these reasons (and a gazillion others), creating healthy workplace relationships is difficult—but it is not impossible, once you have the tools.

Remember your mother's advice about getting along in school? Share. Be nice. Don't argue. If you do not have anything nice to say, do not say anything at all. She actually was on to something there—to get along at work, we just have to reframe her advice a bit:

1. *Share.* Knowledge is power, but only when you spread it around.

2. *Be nice.* Know your own motivations, understand your own reactions, and work to understand others'.

3. *Don't argue.* It is hard to argue with someone who does not argue back.

4. *Don't gossip.*

To get along at the office, we need to use our skills and strengths, build relationships, deliver results, make money, and have fun. To create a work life that incorporates these components, we need a noncompetitive, collaborative approach to working toward both the shared organizational goals and our unique individual personal goals, which may differ from or conflict with those of our colleagues. We also have to move away from defining "being nice" as being an easy target, and we have to characterize kindness as a form of awareness, understanding, strength, integrity, and wisdom. In addition, we have to do away with the old argumentative, right/wrong orientation and the finger-pointing and blame management styles, so that we can allow others their opinion and learn to communicate objectively.

When managing your work life of office politics, bully bosses, and cranky coworkers, you can respond in a way that builds bridges and increases communication, or you can make assumptions from a narrow information base (like the men in the legend) and react with a style that damages your reputation, destroys relationships, and leaves you dreading your workday.

In order to get along in the workplace, you need to develop healthy relationships, become aware of your behavior, and recognize how the opinion that others hold of you may differ from your intent. Moving through the following chapters, we will take a closer look at how you see yourself, how others see you, the differing styles with which you react and communicate, and how to shift to a more effective style under some challenging circumstances.

I

My Boss Hates Me

I was fired from my very first job. I was 18, a clerical assistant in the traffic department of an equipment manufacturing business in Palo Alto, California. After I had been working for the company for a few months, my boss decided to terminate the traffic department secretary to whom I was an assistant. It was determined that after 17 years in her job, this woman was not working out. My boss also decided that I could take her place and do my job, too—at my same pay rate (minimum wage). I told my boss that doing two full-time jobs was impossible, but he was quite adamant that it was not only possible but required. This was my first experience in disagreeing with my boss about expectations.

The second disagreement came when I said to the same fellow, "No one can do a good job if they're doing the work of two

4

people at one time. If you want a half-assed job, you'll just have to hire a half-assed person to do it." That was about the same time he decided he did not really like me. Chalk it up to youthful indiscretion—I was outta there.

How Do You Know?

In some cases, as in mine, your boss may tell you directly that your behavior or performance does not meet the expectations of the job. When you receive this information, as I did at the ripe age of 18, you can choose to be upset, or you can choose to learn the skills you need in order to shift your style and results, technically and behaviorally, to match the objective.

Some bosses may be subtler in their approach. You might notice that your boss does not have time for you, or takes every opportunity to highlight your errors, or drops hints to your colleagues, subordinates, or management about your shortcomings. Whether you've made a huge behavioral blunder like mine, or you simply have a sense that your boss dislikes you, it's time for you to take control, assess your work style and your career path, and make some positive changes to rebuild your reputation.

Mistakes We Make

Raj was a techno-genius. As project director for a dot com, Raj worked magic with his computer, creating technically precise solutions for his team. Unfortunately, his solutions were so user-unfriendly that the team did not understand them and the firm's clients could not use them. Raj was a perfectionist who did not like having his work examined or altered, and he made this clear to anyone who dared to question him. Team members complained to the VP about Raj, and after several sessions with his boss and human resources, Raj could not deny that his team and his boss found him inflexible and stubborn. However, he feared that the only way he could repair his relationships—and his reputation—was to surrender his product excellence, and he was not willing to make that sacrifice.

Clues We Receive

Although Raj recognized that the team found his work *product* complex and even unworkable, he did not realize that the members of his team were also uncomfortable with his work *style*— that is, not until he was told. He had not noticed that his boss and the other members of his team cringed in his presence or simply avoided him; he had not noticed that his boss would not make time for him; and he had not noticed when team members, with his boss's approval, went to outside sources for client solutions that Raj was more than qualified to create. He had missed every subtle and not-so-subtle clue.

When his boss presented him with a formal 30-day performance improvement plan, Raj read the comments concerning his harsh and demanding behavior, and initially chose to internalize them as limitations of the people with whom he was working. He was less than 30 days away from losing his job when he contacted me for coaching. He realized he was going to lose his job, and he was ready to make some changes.

How to Get Out and Stay Out of Hot Water

It is true that people relate, or disengage, for reasons that sometimes escape us—but having a good relationship with your boss is one relationship that you cannot let slide.

Once Raj determined that he wanted to fill the gap between his current behavior and behavior that would move him forward in his career, our coaching sessions focused on three fundamental areas of skill development: self-awareness, receiving feedback, and motivation.

1. Self-Awareness

Self-awareness is the single most important factor in getting along in your career and your life. It is your ability to understand *why* you do what you do.

When you are self-aware, you know and understand yourself, including your own reactions; because of that, you tend to make better choices. Without self-awareness, you tend to repeat old patterns, ignore your intuition, and miss the clues and signals you get from others about the impact of your actions and your words.

When you are self-aware, you recognize the connection between what you feel and what you think, do, and say. Self-awareness is the dot-to-dot of your life—to complete the puzzle, you must understand that your emotions and your behaviors are related.

Connecting the Dots

The dots you need to connect start with your own personal values (in addition to your skills and strengths). Since the term *values* is often used synonymously with needs, or wants, or priorities, let's clarify the way the term is used here.

Things you *want* are things that you can do without; you may want a new car, but you can get along fine without it. You probably do not experience any behavioral changes if you do not get the things you want, but having them makes you happy.

Things you *need* are necessities. In addition to physiological needs (food, air, and water), we each have personal needs, perhaps to be loved, to be acknowledged, to be well regarded, or, as in Raj's case, to control. When your needs are met, you are comfortable, and you are able to focus on your values. When your needs are not met, your behavior changes.

Things you *value* are events, activities, or preferences that you feel are significant, and that you have probably found interesting and fun throughout your entire lifetime. If your value is to create, you will be at your most energized and fulfilled when you are working in an environment that allows you to use your creativity. If your workplace does not honor your value to create, you may feel unfulfilled or bored, but it is unlikely that your behavior will change.

Raj chose to let his need overshadow his value. His need for control was so strong that when he received feedback, he forgot about the value he held in order to be an expert. His need was not met, and his behavior changed—that is, until he understood his needs and found methods to handle them outside of the workplace. Only then could he focus on his values.

What Is in Your Way?   If there are situations in your career or your life that cause you to behave differently (to dig in your heels, get angry, hide, argue, or cry), take the time to complete this needs identification and elimination process for yourself. Use the Needs Worksheet (Exhibit 1-1) to identify, analyze, and manage your needs. Start by discovering what your needs are, then complete the Needs Analysis Form (Exhibit 1-2) for each need you have selected. Be honest with your needs identification, and be complete in your analysis of how your behavior changes when your need is not met.

Exhibit 1-1
Needs Identification List

Choose your top five needs from the following list, then go to the Needs Analysis Form (Exhibit 1-2) to identify how each affects your career and your life.

_____ Financial security	_____ To be safe
_____ Perfection	_____ To be saved
_____ Prosperity	_____ To be seen
_____ To accommodate	_____ To be self-reliant
_____ To achieve	_____ To be stable
_____ To affect others	_____ To be strong
_____ To be accepted	_____ To be taken care of
_____ To be accurate	_____ To be thanked
_____ To be acknowledged	_____ To be the center of attention
_____ To be appreciated	_____ To be understood
_____ To be approved	_____ To be useful
_____ To be autonomous	_____ To be valued
_____ To be busy	_____ To be well liked
_____ To be calm	_____ To be well regarded
_____ To be cared for	_____ To be worthy
_____ To be clear	_____ To communicate
_____ To be comfortable	_____ To control
_____ To be commanding	_____ To correct others
_____ To be deliberate	_____ To deliver results
_____ To be devoted	_____ To demonstrate authority
_____ To be encouraged	_____ To dominate
_____ To be heard	_____ To follow
_____ To be helped	_____ To get attention
_____ To be helpful	_____ To give
_____ To be honest	_____ To gossip

_____ To be important	_____ To have a cause
_____ To be included	_____ To have balance
_____ To be independent	_____ To improve others
_____ To be liked	_____ To influence others
_____ To be loved	_____ To lead
_____ To be loyal	_____ To please others
_____ To be needed	_____ To prove myself to others
_____ To be noticed	_____ To receive
_____ To be obeyed	_____ To receive compliments
_____ To be powerful	_____ To receive credit
_____ To be praised	_____ To receive loyalty
_____ To be respected	_____ To understand
_____ To be right	_____ _____
_____ _____	_____ _____
_____ _____	

Exhibit 1-2
Needs Analysis Form

For each need selected from the Needs Identification List, complete the following worksheet.

Need # ____ _____

1. I have noticed my need for this need in the following situations:

_____

_____

_____

_____

2. When my need for this need is *met*, I feel

_____

_____

_____

3. When my need for this need is *unmet*, my behavior changes in the following ways:

_____

_____

_____

4. While I'm focusing on getting this need met, I am unable to focus on these important values, strengths, and growth opportunities:

_____

_____

_____

5. Why do I have this need? What "causes" it?

_____

_____

_____

6. What are the costs to me of not having this need met (financial, emotional creative, etc.)?

_____

_____

_____

7. What are the benefits to me (payoffs) of *not* having this need met(adrenaline rush, victim or martyr stuff, energy, ego, etc.)?

_____

_____

_____

8. What will having this need met allow me to do?

_____

_____

_____

9. What do I need to learn or in what way do I need to change or grow in order to get this need met? (List skills to learn, behaviors to shift, negative thoughts to eliminate.)

_____

_____

_____

10. Who can help me meet this need (friend, mentor, coach, therapist, minister)? What do I need from each of these people? (List name and assignment.)

_____

_____

_____

Now move on to the identification of your values, using the Values Worksheet (Exhibit 1-3). You will find that words will jump off the page at you—the start of values identification. Narrow your list down to five values, and for each, ask yourself,

- Where in my life are these values honored?

- What can I do to bring more of these values into my life and career?

Once you have identified your values, you will know what is important to you beyond your technical abilities. Once you have identified your needs, you will have a sense of the barriers you may experience in your workplace—or your personal life. This is the road to connecting the dots of self-awareness: discovering blind spots.

People who are self-aware know that they have weaknesses, and know that they may have difficulty seeing certain of their own weaknesses or limitations. If you believe that self-improvement is a good thing, then learning about how others perceive you is valuable.

Exhibit 1- 3
Values Worksheet

Choose your top 10 values from the following list (or add your own to the list). You are your values, so take your time in selecting those that truly fit. Be honest, and choose only actual values (not things you want or need).

_____ Adventure	_____ To feel good
_____ Danger	_____ To have fun
_____ Excellence	_____ To have impact
_____ Exhilaration	_____ To improve
_____ Family	_____ To influence
_____ Ingenuity	_____ To inform
_____ Originality	_____ To inspire
_____ The unknown	_____ To instruct
_____ Thrill	_____ To invent
_____ To accomplish	_____ To lead
_____ To assist	_____ To learn
_____ To attain	_____ To nurture
_____ To attract	_____ To perceive
_____ To be accepting	_____ To perfect
_____ To be aware	_____ To persuade
_____ To be connected	_____ To plan
_____ To be expert	_____ To provide

_____ To be part of the community	_____ To relate
_____ To be passionate	_____ To relate with a higher power
_____ To be sensitive	_____ To risk
_____ To be spiritual	_____ To rule
_____ To build	_____ To see
_____ To cause	_____ To sense
_____ To contribute	_____ To serve
_____ To create	_____ To set standards
_____ To design	_____ To show compassion
_____ To detect	_____ To strengthen
_____ To discover	_____ To support
_____ To distinguish	_____ To teach
_____ To educate	_____ To touch others
_____ To encourage	_____ To unite
_____ To energize	_____ To use imagination
_____ To enlighten	_____ To win
_____ To experience	_____ _____
_____ To experiment	_____ _____
_____ To feel	_____ _____

2. Receiving Feedback

Welcoming feedback is a method for seeing that continuous improvement remains on your agenda. If you can move beyond taking feedback as criticism, if you can move beyond asking for feedback when you want to hear only praise ("Do I look fat in these jeans?"), then you are moving toward seeing feedback as a tool to help you learn and grow.

When we receive feedback, we have a choice. When the feedback is provided in a positive and respectful way, we can accept it and learn from it. If the feedback is provided in a negative way (more as a weapon), we can enforce a boundary around the presentation of it, and still seek the underlying value in what was shared. Here are four suggestions for being more polished when accepting feedback:

- *Listen.* It is important that you hear what is being said, and it is impossible to do that if you are busy defending yourself. Listen without interruption, denial ("It wasn't me!"), defensiveness ("Yes, but"), deflection (changing the subject), accusing (turning the table), excuses, or justification. Do not react, just respond.

  If you have ever sent a flame email, you have reacted. If you have ever snapped at an employee, peer, or family member, you have reacted. If you have ever picked up the phone to give that so-and-so a piece of your mind, you have reacted. If you have ever replayed a personal or professional interaction and wished you "hadn't said that," you have reacted.

  A reaction is automatic and unthinking, needs based, and limiting. A response requires time to consider and evaluate, clarify and understand. When you give yourself permission to respond, you immediately create more options for yourself. You can still send a flame, you can still snap at people, you can still blast someone by telephone, and you can still let'em have it. But you can also take some time—a few minutes, an hour, a day—before you take any action in these situations, to honor your own values, respect others (even when they're wrong), and maintain your professional reputation at the same time.

- *Clarify.* Get as much information as possible. Be sure to get specific examples so that you completely understand.

- *Acknowledge.* Let the feedback messenger know that you have heard the feedback by thanking her or him for sharing the info with you (even if you do not agree with it). Then review what you have heard on your own time, and consider what it means to you and whether (or how) you can incorporate it into your life.

- *Circle Back.* Make the time to get back to the feedback messenger to let him or her know what you plan to do about the feedback. Make the messenger "right" if that is the case.

Initially Raj was focused on getting his needs met, so feedback was painful for him. He has since learned how to connect the dots between his unmet needs and his behavior, and he can now accept and use quality feedback. He chose to identify and change his less-than-effective behaviors so that he could begin to build more productive work relationships. Raj also found that accepting feedback helped him create an environment of motivation for himself and his team.

3. Motivation

Demonstrating to your boss and your team that you are motivated is one of the keys to rebuilding your damaged reputation.

Motivation has four parts: striving to improve yourself, a commitment to the team vision and goals, initiative, and optimism. These four parts are inseparable. If you are dedicated to improving yourself and committed to your team, but you lack initiative, you are not seizing opportunities that may be just out of sight. If you are dedicated to improving yourself, are committed to your team, and demonstrate initiative, but you lack optimism, you are missing the ability to unite people toward a vision for the future; setbacks and obstacles can seem huge and overwhelming.

Review the needs and values work you did earlier in this chapter to assess your dedication to self-improvement. If you find that you lack the elements of motivation—dedication to self-improvement, commitment, initiative, and optimism—you may also find that your needs are not being met, or that your values are not being honored. Take control of your career, and find whatever is missing for you.

Important Information to Remember before Beginning Your Rebound Plan

Optimism is a learned behavior. Optimism is about your tendency to expect the best possible outcome. The main difference between optimists and pessimists is how they explain setbacks to themselves: An optimist will assume that he or she is empowered to do something to change the negative situation, and a pessimist is likely to assume that there is nothing that he or she can do that will make any difference at all. Optimists believe that negative circumstances are temporary, and pessimists see negative circumstances as permanent. Perhaps it is just the optimist's willingness to take action to change that makes the difference, but you need to know that you have the ability to increase your level of optimism and that if you do so, you will experience increased motivation and improved achievement and also an elevated mood and sense of well-being.

Create Your Rebound Plan

Your rebound plan is your strategy for undoing any damage, creating and maintaining a healthy reputation in your organization, and staying out of trouble. If you have received a formal written notice from your boss outlining your deficiencies, you have a sense of your new targets and objectives. If you are creating your rebound plan based on only your observation or perception of the need for such a plan, then additional work will be required. In either case, on a blank sheet of paper, answer the following questions:

1. Why do you do the work that you do?

2. What have been your main accomplishments? Does your boss see these accomplishments the same way you do? If not, why not?

3. What have you enjoyed the most about this job?

4. What have you enjoyed the least about this job?

5. What is your key motivator? Is this tied to a value or a need, and if so, which value and which need?

6. What is your relationship with your boss? List the top three assumptions, with examples, that your boss makes about you. How did your boss come to this conclusion? What does your boss need to learn about you in order for these assumptions to change?

7. What is your relationship with others? List the top three assumptions, with examples, made by each person with

whom you have a relationship that requires restoration. How did these individuals come to see you in this light, and what do they need to learn about you in order for these assumptions to change?

8. What is the environment (culture) in your organization, and how does that match or contrast with your needs or values?

9. What are your professional/business goals for the next year, 5 years, 10 years?

Your responses to questions 1, 8, and 9 refer to your motivation and commitment to yourself and the organization. Your responses to questions 2, 3, and 5 validate your dedication to self-improvement, your initiative to make it happen, and your confidence that your plan will succeed. Your responses to questions 4, 6, and 7 reveal to you what needs to be fixed, and with whom.

Earn Your Reputation   To rebuild your standing in the workplace, take a deep breath, be willing to take the time required to regain others' trust, and maintain your optimism. Select the approach that will work best for you and the people you are working with.

1. *Rebuild trust.* Trust is a fascinating thing. While it is probably the most important component of a successful relationship, it is not easy to define (or to create) because it is a subjective interpretation of how you feel about someone's behavior.

   When you are rebuilding a shattered workplace

trust, you are trying to convey that you acknowledge
your error (in judgment or behavior), that you do share
similar values, that you do walk the talk, and that you
will be respectful and professional. This process takes
time, and it will not happen on your time schedule—
it will happen on theirs.

You are fighting the perception of your predictability. For Raj, his boss and teammates predicted
that he would always be harsh and hostile. Raj needed
to start with his boss, acknowledging that he had
demonstrated some pretty bad behavior, and that he
had prepared a plan to ensure that the behavior (or
error) would not recur. Here is an example of the apology and rebound kick-off that Raj used:

"I want you to know and see the quality and professionalism I expect from myself. Recently you have
experienced something less than that professionalism—
my surly attitude has been uncalled for and unacceptable. I have allowed my emotions to dictate my actions,
even though I know that this type of behavior is not
appropriate. I take full responsibility for my actions,
and I will make things right. I hope that you will accept
my apology, and that you will allow me to rebuild your
trust and the trust of our team."

2. *Be humble—but do not grovel.* To be humble when you
   are launching your rebound plan is to be accountable
   and responsible for your actions, and willing to work
   at rebuilding relationships.

   To grovel is shame-based, and while you may not
   look back on your own behavior with pride, pleading
   for forgiveness will not support your case.

3. *Work on the process of change.* If you are repairing broken trust or rebounding from a huge error, ask your boss what steps you can take to inspire confidence and trust. This will allow you to focus on and demonstrate your new behaviors, the process of change. Shifting your behavior, and the assumptions that people have about you and your behavior, will not happen overnight.

   If you have been demoted or stripped of special duties, accept this gracefully; work hard, make smart choices, and do well.

4. *Keep learning.* When you are working to repair your relationship with your boss, make certain that you know your value to the organization. Make certain, too, that you continue to learn more about your industry, your company, your job, and your own skills. Every time you learn a new skill, celebrate a new win, achieve a new accomplishment, or receive a message or note of congratulations or thanks, save it in your "Attaboy" or "Attagirl" file. In lean times, you can remind yourself of your contribution and value to the organization, and in better times, you will have a resource when it's time for your next review.

5. *Keep an open mind.* Sometimes the assumptions that others have about you will be too deeply held to change, requiring you to modify your strategy. I once had a boss tell me, in response to my own rebound proposal, "A leopard never changes his spots." His statement spelled out the fact that he was not interested in working with my recovery plan or with me; therefore, I created an exit plan instead, and moved on.

Final Thoughts

If you find that your boss thinks poorly of you, there is no easy way out. Either it is about you, or it is about him or her—and in either case, it's still about you. There is no way out of a poor relationship with anyone, including your boss, without a strong sense of self-awareness. Without such a sense, you may be tempted to deny your accountability, deflect your responsibility, or disengage from the relationship altogether.

Take the time to learn what is in your way. While having a difficult relationship with your boss may not be entirely *your fault*, it is impossible to determine that without first identifying exactly what is missing. Take a close look at your key result objectives, your performance against those objectives, and your behavior. Learn about your own needs and values, and get clear on how your behavior changes when your needs are unmet. Maintain or buff up your self-awareness, motivation, and optimism; learn how to accept feedback; and create your plan to rebuild the damaged relationship.

Sometimes there is just no repairing the broken trust or restoring lost credibility, but even if you sense that this is the case, do not throw in the towel until you know for sure. Seek out an objective viewpoint from a coach. A good coach will help you clearly see what is missing, identify and get over your hurdles, and decide how to proceed—all the while maintaining objectivity and confidentiality. (See the resource section of Chapter 15 for coach referrals to fit any budget.)

If you are comfortable talking over your situation with an internal mentor, a human resources representative, or a close friend, try that. Remember, though, that an internal mentor, human resources representative, or friend may be less than objective in her or his view of what you have experienced. As you speak with such a person, make it clear that you are looking for objective and constructive feedback and recommendations, that you want confidentiality maintained, and that you are not just looking for solace or consolation.

Once you are certain you have reached the point of no return, see "When All Else Fails" in Chapter 13.

Strategies and Concepts to Remember

1. Take the time to learn your values—they are who you are.

2. Understand your needs—those things that are in your way.

3. Learn the difference between what you value, need, and want.

4. Become self-aware—know what you are feeling and why, and how it appears to others.

5. Be open to positive feedback as a tool for growth and learning, and be prepared to enforce a boundary around any feedback that is negative, hostile, or confrontational.

6. When communicating with anyone, avoid denial, deflection, or defensiveness.

7. Build a reputation that is accurate and positive.

8. Earn trust, don't demand it.

9. Be humble, but don't grovel.

10. Accept change—it will happen whether you like it or not.

11. Understand that others may see you differently from the way you see yourself.

12. Learn to learn, and learn to enjoy learning.

2

When You Work for a Jerk

Philip Topham, a senior information management executive and coaching client, shared his early-career nightmare boss story with me:

> *None of us knew whether the boss would arrive in his Ferrari or his Custom Jeep. When he arrived in his Ferrari, it was not a good sign.*
>
> *Like a precision Doo Dah Parade of one, on a Ferrari day he would arrive after 9:00 A.M., screech into the parking lot, leap from the car, and with briefcase in one hand and the Wall Street Journal in the other, march into the office, head straight, chin up—no smiles; no hellos.*
>
> *His office door would close, and 3 minutes later the door would fly open. "You F##$#$%# pieces of @$#@$ . . . #$%#*

#$ . . . #@$%#$ . . . get on the phones, bring me some deals, you lazy @#$@#$, I should fire you all."

This was his idea of a motivational speech, and it would last for several minutes. Like cockroaches in the light, we scuttled back to our phones; he would return to his office, not to be seen again until his next tirade.

When we knew the coast was clear, we would crawl back to the water cooler and ask each other how the job search was going.

How can you work for someone whose leadership style is so unbalanced? Philip knew that this situation was not good for him, and he moved on. What would you do? Or, better yet, what have you done when you were faced with this predicament?

When you find that the results of your interview process did not adequately predict the reality of the workplace, it is time to analyze what is not working for you, and deal with it.

Leadership Styles

There are many leadership styles, ranging from decisive to coercive, from collaborative to inert, and everything in between. While there is no single style that fits all occasions, there are certain characteristics that are demonstrated by an authentic leader, regardless of style:

- Listening before acting, knowing that he or she doesn't have all the answers

- Providing direction, creating and supporting a vision, mission, and purpose for him- or herself and the organization

- Creating an environment of motivation and support of others, while also always looking for a better way

- Showing respect and encouragement (rather than engaging in ridicule and finger-pointing) for those who are willing to try new things, even if they occasionally fail

- Supporting continuous learning and self-renewal

- Leading by example and honoring a set of values that remain constant

- Demonstrating high personal and professional standards, and appreciating the richness of a diverse workforce

- Making and keeping commitments

- Sharing decision making with others throughout the organization and understanding the difference between strength (effective action) and power (desire to dominate)

Finding that your new boss is lacking in some of the finer points of leadership can be a challenge, especially if he or she demonstrates one or more of the Four Deadly Management Styles: the Bully, the Know-it-all, the Incompetent, and the Micromanager.

The Bully Boss

There are bosses who are demanding but kind; there are bosses who are well intended but lacking in self-awareness; and then there are Bully bosses. Bullies sometimes use a pattern of small and subtle actions over an extended period; each individual deed may not seem abusive, but the cumulative effect makes the situation unbearable. Other Bully bosses are constantly pushy, hostile, angry, rude, blaming, threatening, attacking, and inclined to erupt in a fit of rage.

During the high-tech boom of the 1990s, talent was hard to find, and some people were promoted beyond their abilities. The economic downturn that followed encouraged those ill-equipped individuals to push harder in order to prove their worth to their organizations.

Thus, the Bully:

Ron was recruited away from a small software company in the Southwest into a more senior position with a larger software firm in the Northeast. After the first few weeks of indoctrination and assimilation into the new company and its culture, Ron was invited to a monthly leadership team meeting. Ron's peers at the SVP level, his boss and his boss's peers at the EVP level, and the president of the company were all in attendance. After Ron was introduced and welcomed, the president asked him a question. Consulting his notes, Ron began to respond, but the president abruptly cut him off: "You don't know what the hell you're doing! I'll call [the client] and get the answer myself!" he shouted. "I don't know why we hired someone so stupid!" Welcome to your new company, Ron.

Ron was humiliated in front of his peers and senior management, and because he had not been clued in about the president's Bully style, he concluded that he was a failure in his new job. After the meeting, however, Ron spoke with his boss and his closest peers, and he realized that at one time or another, everyone in the room had been on the receiving end of the president's brutal behavior. He heard stories about those who stood up and challenged the boss, those who shied away and tried to avoid him, and those who threw in the towel and quit.

Ron considered his own, similar options: He could fight back (not his style), he could try to hide (also not his style), or he could change the way he responded to, and internalized, the boss's behavior. He chose the last option.

Ron realized that he really liked his job and the company, and he was willing to work with his boss, his colleagues, and the president to create a communication process that would work for them. He identified his needs, values, and basic style, and he created a communication style plan that he shared with each of his leadership colleagues, including the president. It included an assessment of his value to the organization, a review of key results and motivations, and a section on "how I'm best managed." Since doing this, Ron has not been a target of harassment or humiliation.

The Know-It-All

Your boss has been there, done that, and told you all about it at every opportunity. This type of manager believes her- or himself to be an all-around expert, and will typically stick to doing things exactly the way they have always been done in an effort to eliminate surprises and ensure consistent, although not stellar, results.

This is another insecurity disguise: In an effort to appear as a powerful authority, this person will make sure of being seen as all knowing. Because these managers demand followership from their team, they tend to discourage new processes or ideas, or to pinch the good ideas or accomplishments of others:

Brett is the seasoned general manager of a diversified service organization. He joined the leadership team in August, following his repatriation to the United States after several years in the United Kingdom. During the first few months of his employment, Brett came to suspect that his boss, Jon, expected huge increases in service results—without changing anything. Jon told Brett several times that the processes and people that were in place, the way things were being done, and the people who were doing those things were "right," and that if Brett were only a better GM, he would deliver the results expected.

The final straw for Brett came after a new client signing. Brett had changed an approach and several processes and had offered expanded services to a new client—and the result was the biggest contract the company had ever seen. Brett was pleased and proud of his team and their work, and he sent a memo to Jon outlining their accomplishment. Jon immediately sent an almost identical memo to corporate headquarters, with copies to all employees, identifying this new client signing as his own win (with no mention of Brett or his staff).

Brett had several options: He could confront Jon, asking for acknowledgment of the accomplishment and any future accomplishments; he could make sure that all future announcements on client signings were sent to corporate headquarters and to Jon *at the same time;* and he could reevaluate working for a boss with these tendencies. Brett decided to do all three. He first confronted Jon, asking for appropriate acknowledgement in the future, and he then made sure that each client win was broadcast to the company under his own name. Then, finding that the energy required to "watch" Jon was more than he was willing to expend, Brett started a job search campaign to find a position that was more closely aligned with his own values.

The Incompetent

It is difficult to work for someone when you are continually distracted by the depth of his or her incompetence. Unfortunately, people are sometimes promoted beyond their abilities—and in a competitive landscape, if you are overlooked for promotion into a position that an incompetent now holds, you may find the situation even more aggravating.

> *Diane was a client relationship director for a relocation services organization. When a corporate restructuring occurred, self-contained business units were created, increasing the manager's span of control under the new title "business unit director." Diane was the only one of her peers who was not chosen for the new position. She was instead told that she would be responsible for training the sales manager, Steve, in the ways of operations, and that Steve would be the new business unit director.*
>
> *Steve did not want to let on that he did not understand operations, and he was not open to learning from Diane. He tried his best to hide his lack of knowledge, yet he was known for making promises to clients that were impossible to keep. The last straw for Diane was when Steve made a commitment to a client to provide a special service at no cost—not realizing that the fee for that service was in fact $25,000. When questioned about how such a foolish mistake could have been made, Steve told his boss that Diane was the culprit. Diane asked Steve why he had blamed her, and he admitted to her that he had indeed made the mistake, that he had indeed blamed her, and that he would do the same thing again to save his job and his reputation.*

Through this episode, Diane learned that the new structure within the organization was not going to work for her—and that her type of incompetent boss knew just enough to keep himself out of trouble, while letting others take the fall.

There are incompetent bosses who realize that they are in over their heads, and they may welcome your help and support. Then there are incompetent bosses who have no clue. This lack of awareness provides you with an opportunity to complain or ridicule, to open the door to discussion and learning, or to make some critical decisions about where your career is headed. One of these choices keeps you stuck, and the others move you forward.

The Micromanager

This manager gives lots of feedback, almost exclusively negative. A micromanager is preoccupied with insignificant tasks, magnifies complaints, issues infinite orders, is devoid of priorities, sends conflicting messages, watches your time, works long hours (and expects subordinates to do the same), is fanatical about paperwork (e.g., a quality report is measured by the pound), uses performance evaluations as weapons, and freely gossips about the shortcomings of others.

Potpourri: Daniel's Story

For several years I have worked for the devil incarnate and his ill-mannered and insensitive minion. He is an intimidating, micromanaging brow-beater, with limited integrity; he enjoys humiliating employees in team meetings, taking credit for work he did not do, and screaming when things do not go his way—and his assistant is just as bad. She "befriends" you in order to get you to open up, and then she uses the information she gains against you. Blame and condemnation is the management style, fear is the reaction—and the problem is, as unhappy as we are, we are in a small town in an industry that is growing, so that even with the poor management style of our leaders, we are showing good bottom-line results. This predicament is wearing me down. I don't know if I should just keep quiet and take it, hoping that someday someone will end this craziness, or whether I should pray for the overdue apocalypse with its ensuing lake of fire event and hope for the best.

Can This Relationship Be Saved?

Before Daniel, Diane, Brett, and Ron began to build strategies to turn their relationships with the boss around, I asked them to consider these three preliminary criteria. To begin a rebound plan:

- You must really like the company—if you don't, why bother?

- You must really like the work you do—if you don't, your wanting to "deal" with your boss may be more about revenge than about repair.

- Your current issues with your boss's behavior must be ongoing for less than 2 years—any longer than 2 years requires a bigger change.
  The next step was to answer the following questions:

- When did you first notice this behavior? Did it begin because of a specific work-related event (e.g., the boss's poor performance appraisal) or because of professional

or personal difficulties (e.g., a demotion or a divorce),
or has the behavior always been present?

- Have you been singled out for mistreatment, or is your
  boss an equal opportunity tyrant?

If the behavior pattern is relatively recent, is derived from a
critical event in the boss's life, and is widespread, your chances
of turning the situation around are good. If, however, the behavior pattern is long-term, constant, and directed at you, there is
work to be done.

Daniel, with the "devil boss," had been employed by his
organization for over 3 years. His boss had always treated Daniel
in this way, and he treated most of the other members of the leadership team in an equally abusive fashion. Although Daniel liked
the company, he found his work unfulfilling, so his decision to
move on was easy. He began a job search campaign, and within
90 days he had accepted a more senior position in an organization with a culture that was more in tune with his values.

Let's Have a Talk

Ron did a great job of confronting the Bully-boss president. Aside
from courage, all he needed was an outline of a plan to work well
together. This type of "talk" is not an aggressive confrontation,
but simply a conversation between two people in search of open-
ness, balance, and integrity. Although both Brett and Diane
decided to move on in their careers, they both addressed their
issues directly with the boss. To restructure your relationship with
your boss, you will ultimately need to sit down and examine your
issue together. First, you need to know what *you* want, and then
you can determine what else might be missing:

- What do you want, why do you want it, and from whom do you want it?

- What has happened, how do you feel about it, and what is at stake here?

- How might you have contributed to the issue?

- How long have your feelings on this issue been building?

- How long have you been postponing this conversation?

- How much have your feelings been undermining your relationship with this person?

Make an outline of what you would like to say. Write it out, say it aloud, and try to hear it as if someone were saying it to you. When you are comfortable with what you have to say and how you want to say it, request a meeting. This talk is not an opportunity for you to express your anger or to blame anyone—this is a way to say what you have seen and experienced, how you feel about it, and how you want to resolve the problem.

Ask your boss if he would be comfortable using a basic conflict resolution format for the meeting—that is, each person in turn states her or his perceptions, while the other person listens quietly to the entire concern, responding or asking questions only when the speaker has finished. This will give you an opportunity to give your examples of situations and recommendations for change without the need to defend your position when questions arise: You are on a fact-finding mission. When you have completely described your concerns, ask your boss for comments or input—and listen carefully, taking notes. Let your boss complete the other side of the story, without interruption. Your boss's version of events may be quite different from yours, so show that you have an open mind by asking "what" questions in order to learn more. Do not be tempted to counter your boss's comments while he or she is speaking; let your boss finish, and remember that the purpose of the meeting is to find out how the two of you can best work together.

Once each of you understands the other's position, it is time to strategize your ongoing action. Ask, "What do we need to do to resolve this?" to identify a resolution. Once you reach agreement, it is time to introduce the boundaries you will use to maintain the agreement.

Standards and Boundaries

The best way to hold people accountable for their behavior is through setting and enforcing boundaries. Boundaries are how you allow other people to treat you, and standards are how you behave toward others. Before you create your new, politically correct, strong boundaries around the boss's behavior toward you, there are a few ground rules:

1. You can't extend a strong *boundary* (e.g., "you may not yell at me") if your personal *standard* on that topic isn't equally as strong (e.g., you can't go around yelling at others).

2. Boundaries are not walls or weapons, but rather a filter to protect you.

3. Setting and enforcing boundaries requires even more courage.

The process of setting boundaries is simple: You decide what behaviors are unacceptable to you. Enforcing boundaries is more difficult. You need to decide what you will do if someone violates your boundary. You have several options for dealing with those who have crossed over the line: inform them that they have done so, make a request that they stop, instruct them to stop, or leave. Here are a few examples that Ron chose as boundaries for his boss:

- *Inform.* "Are you aware that you are raising your voice?"

- *Request.* "I understand the urgency here, and I can hear that you are upset. We decided in our meeting that I'd ask you to rephrase when I felt you were being disrespectful; can you please reframe your concern so that we can continue the conversation?"

- *Instruct.* "We have discussed that I do not allow people to yell at me, and I have asked you to stop. Let's either change the tone of this conversation or continue it later."

- *Leave.* "I've asked several times, and the tone of this meeting isn't changing. I can tell that this is not a good time; I will check back with you later today (or tomorrow), and we will finish up."

The secret to making this work is to enforce your boundaries *before* you become angry. Strong boundaries and even stronger standards for your own behavior will allow you to teach the boss that arguments, backstabbing, interruptions, blame, and finger-pointing are not OK with you.

Setting boundaries is an individual thing. No one else needs to know that you've created them until you enforce them; they are for your protection, your peace of mind. It is wise to create some form of documentation of the boundaries that you have set, when you have enforced them, and with whom. In the event that your boss refuses, directly or indirectly, to respect the boundaries that you have created, you will have a record of your attempts to rectify the situation before moving on to your HR representative.

Final Thoughts on Working with Challenging Leadership Styles

There are many different leadership styles. Good leaders realize that no single approach fits all situations; great leaders use different leadership styles in different situations. Some people are great leaders in training, and when that is the case, one of the most powerful conversations you can have with your boss is one that outlines how you are best managed. Help your boss learn what works for you, how to listen, how to provide direction and support, how to be respectful and encouraging, and how to lead by example. This way, you both win.

Strategies and Concepts to Remember

1. Every great leader employs more than one leadership style.

2. Great, authentic leaders share similar characteristics when it comes to working with others.

3. Some bosses need to learn how to be leaders—and you may be the teacher.

4. Set high standards for your own behavior.

5. Create, and enforce, strong boundaries for how others—including the boss—can treat you.

6. Confronting an issue does not have to be hostile or aggressive.

7. Enforce your boundaries before you become angry.

8. Restructure your relationship with your boss by sharing how you are best managed.

3

Cranky Coworkers

John, a director-level operations manager, wakes up at 6 A.M., goes for a run, takes a shower, gets dressed, and meets his wife and children in the breakfast room for a quick bite and coffee before the start of their day. John asks each of his children about their plans—little Johnny is going on a field trip; little Janie has softball practice after school. Then John and his wife, Jane, share their plans for the day. Jane says, "I'll be presenting an annual review to my biggest client today; wish me luck." John says, "Good luck, honey; I know you'll knock 'em dead. I have a big day too—I'm planning on being an irritating, belligerent, and arrogant pain today."

Getting Up on the Wrong Side of the Bed

Just about every organization has at least one cranky character, ranging from the occasionally annoying to the downright cantankerous. But does anyone go to work intent on holding the title of "office pain"?

Most cranky coworkers do not plan to be difficult. They are simply unaware of their own behavior, just as they are unaware of the impact of their actions and words on others. They also do not realize how harmful their actions may be to their own career success.

Surprisingly, there are understated benefits in their behaviors: All of them are great lessons for us when we think about these encounters as mirrors of our own idiosyncrasies. Often the troublesome behaviors of others reflect back to us our own unattractive behavior. If you are troubled by a complainer, how often do you complain about your own life? If you are blasted by a bully, what aggressive behaviors in your own life need softening? This concept is something to think about as you fine-tune the skills for dealing with the cranky coworker in your life.

In the Hectic Pursuit of Peace of Mind

Do not deny it; we each have an ornery person inside us at times. We can all be overloaded at work, rushed at home, and burdened by a set of external expectations that seem never-ending. If you are struggling to live the "perfect lifestyle," which is possible only with the right car, the right home, the right job, the right physique, and the right beer, you may also be tied to a compulsion to earn, spend, and constantly strive for more of the material things to cover a fear of inadequacy.

This crazy process of unrealistic external expectations can result in our demonstrating a superior attitude at work and at home. I have done it myself, and I became self-righteously angry when the world treated me differently from what I believed was my entitlement. If you are in this cycle, take the time to ask yourself, "How's that working for me?"

I Am Not Irritable!

Just how irritable are you, and what sets you off? Take the Irritability Test (Exhibit 3-1) to determine your IQ score, and check back here for the results.

Exhibit 3-1
How Irritable Are You?

Answer all of the questions using the following scale:

1 point: I would feel a little bothered   3 points: I would feel angry
2 points: I would feel annoyed   4 points: I would feel *furious*

____ In a team meeting, your boss harshly corrects (and embarrasses) you, yet similar actions by your teammates go unnoticed.

____ You are rushed but ready to leave for work, and you find that you do not have enough gas to make it to the corner, much less the office.

____ You are sharing an important issue with someone on the phone, and you can hear that the person you are speaking to is typing on the computer.

____ You and your friend have agreed to attend a concert; you made the arrangements and paid for the tickets, and you are ready to go. That day, your friend calls to say that a dream date has just appeared, and he or she backs out at the last minute, leaving you hanging.

____ You achieve a great success at work, and your boss takes the credit.

____ You are stopped at a red traffic light, and the person in front of you does not notice the light has changed because he is talking on his cell phone. Now you have both missed the green light.

____ Your colleague makes a mistake and blames it on you.

____ You lend someone your favorite book, and she or he does not return it.

____ You are in a serious discussion with colleagues, and one of them will not let you get a word in edgewise.

____ You are running late, but you need to stop at the grocery store for a few items. You have less than 10 items to purchase and you have cash, so you head for the quick-check, 10-items-or-less-cash-only aisle. As you make your way to the queue, another shopper, with at least 15 items in his cart, pushes in front of you. And he has to write a check. And he does not have a pen. And he does not have ID.

____ Total Score

Scoring Key

0–12. If you scored 12 or under, you are either in a perpetual Zen state or in denial. Zen is great; denial is not. Denial is a powerful way to avoid responsibility. The battle cry of the person in denial is, "Don't blame me!" For a professional or executive, this pattern of denial can result in finger pointing and blame management. If you are a professional who is in denial, you may believe yourself to be more flexible, responsible, trustworthy, and credible than others may observe you to be. Know your emotional status, and face your strengths and limitations with an eye toward learning, growing, and improving yourself and your life.

13–24. If you scored in this range, you have found a way to practice awareness and self-awareness. You know what is going on around you, and you understand what is going on inside of you. You have self-respect, and you demonstrate respect and empathy for others. You have learned to detach—you do not take people personally, and you do not take their problems, including denial, personally.

25 or over. If your score was over 25, your reactions to life's difficulties and aggravations may be more angry or aggressive than the average. If you find you experience repeated angry reactions that do not quickly soften, you may have the reputation of having a very short fuse—and being an anger machine is not good for the reputation.

Anger at Work

It seems that we, as a society, are far angrier than we used to be. A study released recently indicated that nearly 25 percent of American workers often feel "underground chronic anger" on the job, not only because of heavy workloads, but because they feel betrayed or let down by their employers. While anger is a healthy, natural emotion, the distressing reality is that we often see anger expressed through explosive behavior and violence—on the road, in schools, in domestic situations, and at the office. The problem is not anger itself; the problem is the way we express—or mismanage—it.

The Three Big Uglies

Displays of anger can take just about any form, from tears to tantrums, yet in the workplace we actually see only a select few of the possible manifestations. The Three Big Uglies, listed here, are most typically seen in a corporate or office setting. Do you recognize either yourself or your coworkers?

1. Do you blow up at people, threaten, shout or swear, blame others, or break things? If so, you may be showing your need to assert your power over others, you may have a need to be "right," or you may not know how to communicate when you are angry.
   a. If you work with someone who is violent and threatening, verbally or physically, report it to your management or human resources representative. This type of anger is inappropriate in any setting, and it may possibly be dangerous. If your coworker yells, throws things, or blames and verbally bashes you, set a boundary for that person, and let him or her know that you will not tolerate this behavior.
      Boundary setting has two steps:
      • You decide where your personal borders are, and when to enforce them. Establish a list of the behaviors that you will not tolerate.

Most of us find it easy to enforce a boundary to protect ourselves from physical harm; for example, "You may not hit me." Developing strong workplace boundaries around anger might also include

"You may not yell at me."

"You are not allowed to criticize or make fun of me."

- Enforce the boundary. This can be tricky—you must not extend a boundary when you are already angry. Following the process for enforcing boundaries from Chapter 2, you would inform, request, instruct, or leave. When you find that a coworker is close to the point of explosion, to enforce your "no yelling" boundary, you might start with *inform*: "Julie, did you notice that you're starting to raise your voice?"

    If that does not slow the anger machine, move on to *request*: "Julie, I'm not comfortable with your yelling at me—can we take a deep breath and start this conversation over?"

    If Julie maintains her loud and angry style, move on to *instruct*: "I do not allow people to yell at me. Please change your tone, or we can continue this conversation another time."

    Finally, if necessary, *leave*: "I am sorry you are so angry. Since this seems to be a bad time for you, let's get back together when you are ready to talk."

    Setting and enforcing boundaries is simply a process of making those who were unaware of your preferences fully informed of them. As you begin to enforce your boundaries, you will notice a change in the behavior of others toward you, and in the way you think about yourself.

b. If you display your anger in this way, review your personal needs from Chapter 1 and create a strategy to get those needs met. Also, commit to improving your personal standards of behavior, and strengthen your boundaries around how others treat you.

If you find that anger is difficult for you to manage on your own, you may have some unresolved issues that are in need of healing—consider working with a therapist or counselor on some anger management techniques. Your employer's Employee Assistance Program (EAP) will have a list of qualified therapists, or you can contact your health insurance provider for a recommendation. You might also try community services agencies that offer qualified therapists on a sliding financial scale to those in need of healing, so that this service is affordable by everyone. These services will help you learn how to manage your anger.

2. Are you belligerent or overly critical? Do you finger-point, name-call, use sarcasm, or create or spread malicious gossip? If so, you are exhibiting the most common form of workplace anger—yet it is still inappropriate.

a. If you work with someone who behaves this way, create strong boundaries around how you will allow him or her to treat you (see Chapter 2). That way, when an individual tries to assuage his or her anger by belittling you, you can put a stop to it.

b. If you are the aggressive critic, your tendencies may be due to either weak standards of personal behavior or unmet needs (see Chapters 1 and 2). Identify your triggers, and set your boundaries accordingly.

3. Do you withdraw emotionally, give people the "silent treatment," play martyr or victim followed by a temper tantrum, or deny your anger? If so, you may be exhibiting traits of passive-aggressive anger. People with these tendencies often believe that they do not have the right to be angry, believe that anger is inappropriate or childish, believe that they will be disliked if they are angry, or just fear that they may offend someone with their anger.

a. If you work with someone who displays passive-aggressive anger tendencies *that affect you directly*, talk it out with that person. Let the person know how this behavior affects your work, and ask the person how you can help him or her discuss his or her dissatisfaction or disappointment in a more productive way.

b. If you are aware that you display passive-aggressive tendencies, take stock and regroup. Speak directly with the appropriate person (the trigger). Remain calm, focus on the person's behavior by using "I" statements ("I feel angry when X"), stick to the subject at hand, and allow for open discussion. This is managing anger. To do this in a healthy way, we must realize that anger is a basic and normal emotion, and that when we are angry, we are just solving a problem by demonstrating the difference between assertively handling an angry situation and aggressively handling an angry situation.

Any of the Three Big Uglies requires development of stronger standards for our own behavior, enforcement of stronger boundaries for how others are allowed to treat us, and identification and satisfaction of unmet needs (see Chapters 1 and 2).

Managing Anger

Managing anger is a skill that takes practice. Is there a pattern here? Are there specific triggers, either internal or external, that result in your anger? An internal trigger may be a belief that "I must always be right," which requires a reassessment and realignment of your personal beliefs and standards. An external trigger may be your colleague's constant whining or complaining, which will be eliminated through setting—and enforcing—strong boundaries.

We know that mismanaged anger causes stress, conflict, violence, and self-destructive behaviors that can destroy careers, reputations, relationships—and lives. A key for all of us, both personally and professionally, is to identify our anger triggers, identify how deeply we feel anger, and determine how in control (or out of control) we feel when we are angered. Then we can learn the skills that we require if we are to manage our anger. The following process is designed to help you manage your anger:

1. Identify what it is that ticks you off, especially identifying any pattern. Build your sense of awareness by asking yourself the following questions:

a. What am I angry about? When was the last time I got angry? (Alternatively: On what issue, or with whom, do I most often become angry?)

b. Just before I reacted in anger, what was I feeling? Did I feel provoked, fed up, fearful, or _____?

c. How did I react? Was my anger in proportion to the event that triggered it?

d. When have I felt this way before, and what did I do about it then?

To help clarify this Q & A process, let's review Colleen's pattern of anger. Colleen is a customer service representative who is working on a team of service and support people. For the umpteenth time, her support person, Pam, did not make a requested deadline, and Colleen's report to the vice president of operations is going to be late.

Colleen responded to the anger identification questions in this way:

a. *I am angry that Pam made me look like a slacker. The last time I was angry was the last time Pam dropped the ball.*

b. *I was feeling frustrated. She always does this to me! Her work is consistently slow and late. And, since she doesn't report to me, I have no control over her, so I was feeling like a victim of her poor work habits. And I felt ashamed to have to deliver my report to the VP late. Again.*

c. *I reacted by raising my voice (not quite yelling, but definitely letting her hear my anger), and maybe I was sarcastic. I told her to get her act together, and everyone within earshot heard me tell her off. I was really mad—*

> *it seemed reasonable at the time, but looking back, I went a little overboard.*
>
> d. *The last time I was this angry was the last time Pam did this. I yelled at her then, too, but she still is late with my work.*

2. The next step is to eliminate as many of the possible triggers for your anger as you can. For example, set boundaries around the anger pattern that evolves. In Colleen's case, she needed to set a boundary around the work assignments given to Pam.

   a. Since Pam was consistently late, Colleen set her work deadlines 2 to 3 days ahead of the actual due dates. That way, if Pam continued to be late in delivering her work, Colleen would still have a cushion.

   b. In a quiet moment, Colleen asked Pam to provide a daily update, by email, of her progress on Colleen's work, including an estimated time of completion. Pam agreed to let Colleen know when she was behind in her work, so that Colleen could, if necessary, make other arrangements. This boundary removed the probability of a last-minute scramble when Pam was unable to complete her work on time, and it provided Colleen with a system for documenting a performance issue.

3. While you are eliminating your anger triggers, review your needs list from Chapter 1. Often the issues that push your buttons are tied to your needs, and those issues can be identified and eliminated.

4. Remember, when you are setting and enforcing strong boundaries, develop stronger standards for your own behavior.

    Colleen's standards for her own behavior, including the way she deals with her own anger, needed upgrading. Colleen's anger pattern was largely passive-aggressive (victim behavior, followed by a temper tantrum).

The process of managing your anger through boundary setting works well for those with occasional angry reactions. Setting strong boundaries also works well when your coworkers become extremely angry, as seen in Chapter 2 (Ron's speaking with his Bully boss). However, there are some types of deep-seated chronic anger that require the past-to-present issue resolution approach of a therapist rather than the problem-solving, present-to-future approach of a coach. Give yourself the time and space to learn the new skill of managing your anger—and if you find you need some assistance, ask for it. Learning to manage anger, both yours and that of your coworkers, is another way to build better relationships, develop a strong reputation, and control your career.

Personality Conflicts

We often hear workplace communication issues referred to as "personality conflicts," yet that term seems to imply both permanence and blame. Your personality is *who* you are, and your behavior is *how* you act. You may have a winning personality; when you are having a bad day (or experiencing an unmet need), it is your behavior that changes, not your personality.

    Your observable behavior—the *how* of your style—was

learned, and can be unlearned; the negative styles we see in others and in ourselves are both temporary and blameless (yet not without responsibility and accountability).

Have you ever had someone tell you that you were rough, blunt, or rude, when you thought you were being concise and direct? If so, you were on the receiving end of the gap between the intent of your statement (encoding) and the receiver's understanding of your statement (decoding), a common problem in the five-step verbal communication process. In general, we follow this format:

1. The sender gets an idea.

2. The sender formulates the idea into a statement (encoding).

3. The idea is sent to the receiver.

4. The receiver accepts the message (decoding).

5. The receiver sends feedback to the sender.

This simple communication system becomes complicated when we consider the encoding and decoding process, especially the filters (or lenses) that we use when we communicate with one another, including

- Differing frames of reference

- Listening skills

- Personal problems

- Work-related stress

- Anger, fear, or frustration

- Fatigue

- Urgency (yours or theirs)

- Lack of trust

- Competition for power, status, rewards (ego)

- Turf issues

Given these filters, or any one of a thousand others, it is easy to see how our communications with one another can be tricky.

In addition to the filters we use, the personal values we hold, and the technical skills we have learned, we all have core behavioral strengths. In his book *The Emotions of Normal People* (published in 1928), Dr. William Marston defined a theory suggesting that people can be observed to have one of four basic styles: dominant, influential, steady, or conforming. Marston found that people have behavioral tendencies involving each of the four styles, but that they generally display strength on only *one* style, and each individual has communication preferences based on this core area of strength:

A person with a *dominant* style prefers concise, specific, brief, and organized communication, and is irritated by indecision, disorganization, and generalized discussions.

A person with an *influential* style prefers warm, lengthy discussions involving personal factors, and is annoyed by cold, distant lectures.

A person with a *steady* style prefers a collaborative approach, wishes to be asked questions to draw her or him into a conversation, and is frustrated by being pushed for a quick decision or by a lack of cooperation.

A person with a *conforming* style prefers to discuss facts and data, wishes to ask many "why" questions, and is stressed by ad hoc, loud, disorganized discussions with people who don't have enough information to prove their point.

Using Marston's theory, a typical meeting between a person with an influential style (a warm and fuzzy, unstructured talker) and a person with a conforming style (a logical, data-focused analyzer) is problematic before either party opens his or her mouth! Under this theory, to a change-resistant person with a steady style, a strong-willed person with a dominant style who needs commitment and closure will sound like a bully. This means that, without a road map on encoding, decoding, filters, and basic communication styles and preferences, we'd better fasten our seatbelts for a very bumpy ride.

Who, Me?

Communication with coworkers is a journey through a jungle of needs, values, filters, styles, and generational diversity—to say nothing of gender differences, cultural diversity, and corporate philosophy—so it is little wonder that some workplace relationships are not productive. The following examples of cranky coworkers, along with discussions of how to deal with them, will

give you a chance to look for the lesson while building bridges
(and your reputation).

The Critic   This person questions your logic, finds flaws with
your arguments, shoots down your suggestions, and tends to be
uncompromising in his or her approach to work and relationships. The good news is that critics can often find problems that
have been overlooked by others—the bad news is that they will
rarely take the action necessary to resolve the problems they find.
An intense worker, even when the situation doesn't warrant it,
the critic seems to operate from a platform of scarcity: Nothing
is adequate, nothing is good enough.

The Solution When Dealing with a Critic   It may be natural
to defend yourself against a critic's complaints, especially in a
meeting, but you should make an effort to separate *yourself* from
your *ideas*, considering any criticism to be about the idea, not
about you. Make sure you understand exactly what the critic has
identified as a problem, and paraphrase it back to the critic. This
way, you let the critic know that he or she has been heard (a key
component in shutting off the criticism).

Be diplomatic and respectful. If you can, find something in
the critic's point of view that you can agree with, and then guide
the conversation away from the criticism. This way, you control
the content of the conversation, without making the complainer
or critic "wrong."

If You're the Critic   Work to build your confidence level, and let
your head and your heart talk to each other. Learn how to shut
off the perfectionist in you while maintaining your quality orientation, and learn to be more accepting of others' ideas and beliefs.

The Bulldozer This individual runs roughshod over his or her colleagues. This style is often closely tied to the need to be right (and the fear of being wrong). This individual tends to make decisions before weighing (or hearing) the facts, may be described by subordinates as a bully, and may show that he or she sees things in black/white or win/lose terms. It is typical for the Bulldozer to be insecure, lacking in self-awareness, and oblivious to the feelings and reactions of others.

The Solution When Dealing with a Bulldozer Do not fight back, and do not lose your temper. Set strong boundaries, and enforce them, but do so only when there is no tension around the situation—and make sure that the person knows that this behavior does not work for you.

If You're the Bulldozer It's time to ratchet it down a couple of notches. An ego (sense of self-worth) is a great thing to have— but if you want to be a great communicator, check it at the door. Soften your approach, lessen the opinions, and be aware of a tendency to speak over others or to be blunt (translation: offensive). A good coach can help you become more careful with details, more consistent with decisions, and more patient and concerned with your coworkers—and yourself.

The Quiet Type This individual is typically silent in meetings, speaks only when spoken to, and will withdraw rather than contribute feedback. Highly introverted, the QT coworker may be frustrating because you don't know how to "read" him or her, and he or she may not tell you even when asked. It's not that QTs don't *feel* emotion; it's that they don't display it. Here's a typical conversation between a QT and a coworker:

QUESTION FROM COWORKER: "I hear your cat died yesterday; how are you feeling?"

RESPONSE FROM QT (*monotone*): "Oh, fine."

QUESTION FROM COWORKER: "I hear you just won $400 million in the lottery; how are you feeling?"

RESPONSE FROM QT (*monotone*): "Oh, fine."

The Solution When Dealing with a QT   To draw out a QT, ask open-ended questions, preferably starting with "what," "how," or "why." Then be silent, allowing the QT time to formulate an answer. If the QT doesn't respond, give some help: QTs are typically shy and need time to process information.

If You Are a Quiet Type   If you find that you have QT qualities, work to become more assertive and decisive, and while you naturally find comfort in sameness, learn to rely less on the routine. Focus on your strengths and your values; learn to be comfortable with risk and change (see "The C-Word: Change" in Chapter 5). Learn the skill of shameless self-promotion (see Chapter 8), and learn to participate in discussions without fear of the unknown, of conflict, or of being disliked.

The Accommodator   This person is a hard worker, is sociable, and is people-oriented—so much so that she or he finds it difficult to actually say the word *no*. This "disease to please" leads to a pattern of overpromising and underdelivering, along with a reputation for unreliability.

For Accommodators, saying, "No, I won't have time to help you with your project this week" is indistinguishable from saying, "No, I won't help you because I don't care about you or your project. I'm selfish, and I'm not a team player." Accommodators end up being victims of their own behavior by overextending themselves in an effort to be helpful.

The Solution When Dealing with an Accommodator   Help the Accommodator by talking over and analyzing pending projects, looking for potential roadblocks in advance. Then agree on deadlines, and ask the Accommodator how often he or she would like to check in in order to stay on track. Give the Accommodator an opportunity to say no, or to shuffle priorities with your assistance.

If You Are the Accommodator   Learn how to say no. Try these "no" phrases on for size:

- *Just say no:* "No, I'm unable to help you out this time." Period.

- *The genteel no:* To express your appreciation for having been asked, you might say, "I appreciate your asking me, but I'm not able to do it."

- *The "I'm sorry" no:* "I'm sorry, I am so busy right now, I'll have to say no."

- *The "but I know someone who will" no:* "I don't have the time to help you, but let me recommend someone else I know."

- *The "reprioritize" no:* "You've asked me to complete several top-priority projects by Friday—which of these is most urgent for you, and which can wait until next week?"

The Thief The Thief is always on the lookout for opinions and ideas that can be liberated, renamed, and presented as original work. Victims of thieves find themselves astounded when they hear from their colleagues or bosses that their very own ideas were "inspired recommendations" created by the Thief. Thievery can also occur with written projects, articles from your office—and even your lunch.

During the turmoil of joining two disparate workplaces into one, Gwen, an HR director, found that there was a lunchtime bandit in the office. The bandit, who was never caught, would go to the lunchroom in mid-morning and take one bite out of a sandwich, or one scoop out of a container of yogurt, or one bite out of an apple, and return the uneaten portion from whence it came. This bandit took enough bites here and there to have an entire meal! When the employees arrived in the lunchroom to eat, they were surprised and disgusted by finding a partially eaten lunch.

The Solution When Dealing with a Thief Once burned, as the saying goes. If you have experienced the loss of an idea or a report—or a lunch—at the hands of a Thief, learn from the experience. Simply complaining that "someone stole my idea" won't win you any respect. While it is never good to get into an argumentative "you stole from me" discussion, it's important that you hold a discussion with the Thief to let him or her know that you understand what happened, and that you won't let it happen again. Going forward, limit your discussions with the Thief to neutral and insignificant topics (and keep your lunch in your desk).

If You Are the Thief It's time to do an integrity check. Integrity is a blend of soundness, incorruptibility, and, in this case, honesty. If you are not reliable and dependable, if you do not honor a sense of what is right, and if you deceive or lie (including lying to yourself), your integrity is unbalanced and needs improvement. You can work on rebuilding integrity with a trusted friend, therapist, or coach, but you need to develop your personal foundation in order to enhance your standards of behavior.

The Backstabber This individual believes that workplace rewards can be achieved only by discrediting others. Like a spoiled child running to a parent to tattle, the Backstabber offers tidbits about everything from your work habits to your personal life—and they may be twisted versions of the truth or outright lies.

The Solution When Dealing with a Backstabber Take a helicopter view of the Backstabber's behavior (this is difficult)—do not take it personally. When Backstabbers share their point of view in the form of gossip, they are expressing their fears, insecurities, and self-doubt. Once you allow their negative (and often inaccurate) words to touch your own fears about yourself, you are choosing to operate from a position of defense, timidity, and anxiety—not a good way to move forward in your career or your life. If you have fears or doubts about yourself, acknowledge them, and make a conscious decision not to act on them when dealing with the Backstabber. You can enforce a boundary around the Backstabber, and then handle any fear or doubt in a healthy environment outside of the workplace.

Although you may be tempted, avoid revenge at all costs—revenge (the spreading of negative rumors about the Backstabber) will only serve to diminish your reputation. If you retaliate, people will not remember who started the mud-slinging; they'll only remember that both you *and* the Backstabber were immature, nasty, and untrustworthy.

If You Are the Backstabber   This is another example of integrity gone awry. Review your needs from Chapter 1. What is missing for you? Identify your needs, upgrade your standards, and enforce boundaries around behavior that is uncomfortable for you. Watch your tendency to run on adrenaline, and learn to say *about* someone only those things that you would say directly to his or her face.

The Control Freak   This individual insists that everything be done his or her way. The Control Freak will question, complain, and watch very closely to ensure that every task is completed exactly the way the Control Freak would have done it. Control Freaks see themselves as protecting the team from mistakes, yet they are seen as being intense, demanding, relentless, and impossible to please.

The Solution When Dealing with a CF   Accusing the Control Freak of CF behavior will only agitate the situation, allowing the argument to become one of *who* is right, rather than *what* is right. The answer to working with Control Freaks lies in cooperation and negotiation rather than in finger pointing. If you work for or with a CF on projects, always set goals that can be measured. As a way to eliminate any hovering or surprise checkups, agree that you will send each other updates on the progress of your project as appropriate. Since the CF is fearful that you will not do what you say you are going to do, help her or him to relax by letting her or him know that you are on target.

If you work with a CF, but do not share project work, the best way to handle the CF's behavior is to talk it out. Without blame, let the CF know that you understand the concern for quantity, urgency, and excellence. Also, ask what you can do to show the CF that you are reliable and dependable, and not in need of a "watcher." Your CF may be dealing with a fear of being wrong, of failure, or of being out of control in other areas of his or her life, so your reassurance that you are consistent and trustworthy will help the CF move away from you and on to other issues.

If You Are the Control Freak   If you find yourself watching and nitpicking others' work, you may be a Control Freak. If that is you, ask yourself what you need in order to trust the people you work with, and set a strategy for changing your behavior. If you normally hover over others each day and criticize them, take it one day at a time. Your mantra can be, "Just for today, I'll not hover, inspect, or criticize anyone." Then every time you catch yourself breaking your own rule, write it down: What happened just before you acted to control, and why did it require your attention? At the end of the day, count how many control encounters you had that were unnecessary, or the pattern of issues over which you felt the need to control. If you find you're having trouble shutting down the CF feature, you may want to work with a therapist to identify and heal whatever is in your way.

If I Had a Hammer . . .

Motivational and behavioral theorist Abraham Maslow is quoted as saying, "If the only tool you have is a hammer, you will see every problem as a nail." People are so unique, so varied, and so dissimilar that when you attempt to deal with all exasperating, childish, fussy, arrogant, irritating behavior in the same way, you are trying to change a spark plug with a hammer. There are thousands of problems and conflicts in the workplace, and there are thousands of tools and skills that can be used to resolve them.

The most effective way to work successfully with a difficult or irritating coworker is to first clarify the behavior, understand why it irritates you, use whatever degree of truth exists in your coworker's comments (the lesson), and use the most appropriate tools for responding to the behavior in a constructive way.

Guess what—all communication is imperfect! Like great leaders, you need to learn to adapt your communication to the receiver, improve your language and listening skills, question your assumptions and preconceptions, and *relax*. When you do, you will find that you are much more in control of your career and your life.

Concepts to Remember about Cranky Coworkers

1. Anger is a normal emotion.

2. Angry *behavior* is a choice.

3. Learn how to say no gracefully.

4. Let cranky people be cranky; don't take it personally.

5. Style differences can create barriers between people, if we let them.

6. Separate yourself from your ideas and your work product.

7. Let others take the time they need to mentally process information—it is not a matter of intellect, it is a matter of style.

8. Set high personal standards for your own behavior.

9. Set—and enforce—strong boundaries around how others can treat you.

10. The best anger diffuser of all is to breathe.

4

PLOP Culture

Peer-level office politics—PLOP. In a perfect world, individuals receive recognition, salary increases, plum assignments, and promotions based entirely on merit. In the real world, the role that office politics plays in career advancement and success ranges from a minor schmooze factor (e.g., learning how to play golf because your boss does) to selling your soul in exchange for a megastar spot in the boss's eyes (e.g., stealing a colleague's report and claiming it as your own).

As companies grow and change, shrink and implode, job descriptions and job duties are expanded or contracted, results orientation is intensified, and competition for desirable assignments, visibility, acknowledgement, and reward heats up, you will certainly run into individuals who are willing to do anything to get ahead of the pack. Add to this unclear job definitions, subjective performance evaluations, a win/lose culture, and a follow-the-leader orientation, and you have a recipe for an unhappy workplace.

Seven Deadly Sins of PLOP

Whether the economy is strong or weak, as you move up in your profession, the outlook for career growth becomes more limited (think pyramid—there are many positions at the bottom, fewer at the top). With fewer positions available, the "look at me!" behavior begins, demonstrating the downside of office politics. These Seven Deadly Sins are usually individual behaviors, rather than group behaviors (discussed later in this chapter). Have you experienced (or exhibited) one or more of these?

1. *Someone to pick on.* In an environment where there are fewer and fewer upper-level opportunities, you may see the behavior of finding a victim to persecute. Whether you are on the sending end or the receiving end of this sin, it provides a temporary relief for the sender's sense of insecurity, while it plays to the recipient's fear of rejection.

2. *Gossip.* Not all gossip is negative (as in backstabbing). Sometimes it is used to share cheerful and truthful news ("John just told me he got a promotion!"). Sometimes it is used to pass on distressing, yet truthful news ("I heard from David that John is being laid off, and John does not know it yet"). Sometimes it is just tantalizing drivel ("I heard from Mark that John is having an affair with the grocery clerk").

At best, gossip in the office is a way to build intimate relationships. In a politically charged office where knowledge is power, however, being the purveyor of gossip may only serve to decrease your credibility and trustworthiness, and ultimately ruin your reputation. If you share information about someone that you would not say directly to that person's face, you have crossed the line.

3. *Personalize everything.* In a politically active office, feedback comes in many colors. Sometimes it is delivered in a positive and productive way, and sometimes it is not. Allowing any comments or behaviors, whether idle gossip or constructive criticism, to touch you personally makes them part of your life. This will feed your fear of failure or rejection, and keep you from moving forward.

4. *Saying yes when you really want to say no.* Do you say yes to things that you would really rather not do, and then find last-minute excuses to back out (or just not show up)? This is a demonstration of your limited dependability and reliability, integrity, honesty, and maturity. It is also one of the best ways to lose friends, respect, and your job.

5. *Arrogance and abrasiveness.* This sin is a disguise for insecurity, and it gains energy from the fears of others—fear of being wrong, fear of failure, fear of rejection, and fear of being humiliated. Attempting to demonstrate your knowledge or your power by displaying your anger

or showing a total disregard for others is to confuse decisive leadership with your ego.

6. *Whine.* This sin is committed by people who just are not taking responsibility for their lives. People who are always complaining, always expecting the worst outcome for every event, always believing that nothing's ever right, and constantly criticizing their workplace, their coworkers, and their own lives are playing the role of something between a victim and a martyr. While using this behavior may provide you with sympathy, you may also be viewed as immature and unable to handle increased responsibilities.

7. *Proving you are right, no matter how hard you must push.* If you have lived in a "right/wrong" system, being "right" was the equivalent of being good, and not being right (or being "wrong") was the equivalent of being bad. If you believe that all your value and worth is tied to your being right, then being wrong destroys your self-esteem. The result is that you push to be right, even when you are wrong.

Peer-Level Office Politics—Unhealthy Competition

In my coaching practice, I often see examples of the Seven Deadly Sins—sometimes from the recipient's perspective, and sometimes from that of the perpetrator. I have found that, regardless of the emotional reasons behind these sins, the results are usually the same: If your reaction to office politics shows you to be abrasive, whiny, arrogant, blaming, egotistical, or a gossip, you will be perceived as a difficult employee, and you will probably lose your job, especially during a merger, acquisition, or downsizing. Here is an example of several of the Seven Deadly Sins in action:

Julie was a superstar regional vice president of sales in a Midwestern telecom company. After a round of layoffs, the company rewarded Julie by expanding her sales region, leaving her with fourteen states to cover—and she was thrilled.

As the economy improved and business increased, the company decided to add an additional regional VP to the sales staff and peel a few states from Julie's roster.

Ann accepted the new position of regional VP, including relocation from her Oregon home base to Chicago. When she arrived, her new boss assigned Julie to show Ann the ropes, introduce her around, and help make her transition into her new job, new company, and new city as easy as possible.

For Julie, having fewer states to cover meant fewer sales, and fewer sales meant lower commissions. Julie did not support an addition to the sales staff (although she never discussed her opinion with anyone—Sin 4). Julie was also uncomfortable with the threat of a new hotshot, and she became aggressive—even hostile—toward Ann (Sins 5 and 7). Julie eavesdropped on Ann's phone conversations and client meetings by standing near her office door, rifled through her office when she was out, created a wedge between Ann and the shared administrative staff, and even hacked into Ann's computer after hours to see what she was working on and with whom (Sins 1 and 2). Julie wanted Ann out, and she was willing to do whatever it took to make Ann go away.

Julie could have taken control of her reputation and achieved career success by joining forces with Ann, leading to improved status as both a hotshot *and* a team player. Instead, she ended up with a 30-day notice to improve, a severely tarnished reputation, and a need to rebuild multiple relationships as well as her personal credibility.

Office Politics and Teamwork

It is true that office politics can be used by the duplicitous as a way to force their career advancement, but office politics can also be leveraged by savvy professionals with strong boundaries in support of a healthy set of shared values.

When they are constructive, positive internal political structures are a great way to learn about the true power sources, to get a sense of the unspoken goals and direction of the team or company, and, for the purpose of making a valuable contribution, to get a sense of your new boss's behavior and goals.

Positive Office Politics: Use Your Powers for Good, Luke

Luke was a director-level controller for an up-and-coming software development firm. He had been diligent in honoring his value of continuous learning; one of the first things he did was to find a peer-mentor in the management team. This was not easy for Luke, since he was somewhat shy; nonetheless, he asked the director of operations if she would be his internal mentor, and she agreed. They began by meeting once per week to get to know each other, to learn their mutual goals and interests, and to clarify corporate goals and objectives. After a few weeks, they began to invite a different member of the senior leadership team to join them for lunch each week. These luncheons were ad hoc;

there was no real agenda, other than to find out what was important to each VP within the team.

Luke and his mentor often met during the week between their luncheons for "drop-in" discussions where they talked about everything—new initiatives, the economy, trends in the industry, and the goals and objectives of the organization.

At one of their leadership luncheons, Luke learned from the CFO that a new VP of logistics position was being created, and that the CFO thought Luke was the right person for the job.

After only 11 months as controller, Luke was promoted to a VP position. He was in the right place at the right time, and he created that scenario by leveraging the culture of his organization—again, office politics.

Let the Games Begin

No discussion of office politics is complete without coverage of the ever-popular turf wars. While very few people will readily confess that they have instigated or participated in a form of turf war, I have seen a great number of people who have indeed witnessed, engaged in, or been victims of some form of turf war.

Think of your company's organization chart as a map of Bizaro World, with little fiefdoms of sales, accounting, operations, human resources, and so on. Each has its own sovereign leader, its own rules, its own culture, its own territorial boundaries, and even a language all its own. Any change or new initiative, especially in an organization with a right/wrong orientation, is viewed as a territorial invasion. Now, looking at things this way, do you recognize any of these typical, yet destructive, games?

- *The Snub:* Socially excluding an individual in a way that clearly brands him or her an outcast

- *The Squirrel:* Withholding or deliberately misinterpreting information in an effort to prevent any change from moving forward

- *The Duplicitous:* Agreeing up front to take action or cooperate, then waiting until the last minute to back out

- *The Interfering:* Monopolizing all resources (people and time) so that they are unavailable to work on any project involving change

- *The Filibuster:* Holding meeting after meeting, conference call after conference call, in an effort to waste time, so that the desired change cannot even start

These types of games tend to involve groups of employees who *own* decision making, who *own* information, or who *own* influence in an unconstructive, negative terrain. This sets up a very different method for determining who will succeed, who will survive, and who will fall away in an organization. These games feel personal, and that often leads to needs-based reactions, like those described in Chapter 2.

Natalie has a personal need for approval. She is a bright woman who is intent on doing a great job in her new position at an insurance company. She enjoys participation in brainstorming meetings, and she did so in early in her tenure at the company. The questions she asked and the opinions she shared were counter to those of the "in crowd"; as a result, she was branded a traitor and shunned by the majority of her coworkers. Her rejection by her associates conflicted with her need for approval, and her behavior changed from thoughtful and collaborative to victim. She became more and more withdrawn, and she did not speak up in a meeting again.

Strategies That Work in Office Politics

Since office politics can be positive or negative, it is critical that you read and understand the political realities in your own organization. Consider the following strategies to understand and leverage your workplace situation.

1. Think Collaboration, Not Conflict

When it comes to office politics, it is essential to redefine power, control, compromise, and competition through the lens of collaboration rather than conflict.

Power and *control* generally imply having some form of authority over something or someone, exercising restraining or directing influence over someone; you can have power and control over yourself or someone else. In contrast, demonstrating *strength* requires no competition, no aggression, but only the state of being strong—having and using great resources.

Using a prizefighter and a karate master as a metaphor for *power* and *strength,* the prizefighter is power, aggressive and dominant, pushing and demanding; the karate master is strength, working with personal competence, the environment, and increasing personal energy through self-awareness and self-confidence.

Compromise requires mutual concessions—you give up something, I give up something, and we meet somewhere in the middle. The problem with this process is that the middle may not be the best place to be, and that each person has to lose something in order to get there, opening the door to feelings of resentment or anger. *Collaboration*, however, allows you to focus on *what* is right, rather than *who* is right—no one gives up anything. Collaboration calls for each individual to check his or her ego at the door, operate outside of personal unmet needs, and focus on *what* is best.

Competition is defined as a contest between rivals—and that is exactly the problem. While competition has been used for centuries as a motivational tool, it often leads to conflict, forces people to prove that one is better than another, and requires a winner and a loser. With *cooperation,* common goals are determined, and people work together to accomplish them.

Through collaboration, Raj could have saved his reputation; through cooperation, Julie and Ann could have created a sales team that was unbeatable; and through compromise, I would not have been fired from my first job.

Collaboration, Compromise, and Cooperation at Work

David, a bank president for 8 years, had made his bank one of the strongest in the state. George, a member of the bank's board of directors, had disliked David from the start, for reasons unknown to David. Over the years, George had done everything in his power to discredit David's work, including obtaining bank records and pointing out each error, and spreading rumors about David's abilities. Initially David had spent his energy defending his position by arguing, second-guessing George's next move, retaliating, and finally hiding from George.

Once David began a collaborative approach to George, the relationship changed. David engaged George in clarifying and sharing information and resources on their mutual goals, asked him for his input on various projects, kept him updated on developments and events, and included him in additional committee work. Through cooperation and compromise, George was able to shift his critical, conflict orientation into a balanced focus on delivering results.

Shift your focus from win/lose to working jointly with others (not giving in or giving up); shift from defending your position to understanding the style of the political structure and the behavior of others, from pointing fingers and deflecting blame to accepting responsibility for spotting any opportunity to collaborate. Even the harshest critic will find it difficult to argue with someone who will not argue back ("Well, oh yeah?"), defend him- or herself ("Yes, but . . ."), deflect ("Look at John, he is worse than me . . ."), or hide.

You can initiate collaborative behavior by focusing on what is best (rather than on who is right). Asking, "What can we do to work best together?" is a great way to open the door to collaboration. It is difficult to respond to that question with a defensive, grandstanding, or blaming answer; however, if you receive a response that displays anger, use your boundaries to get a handle on the conversation, and move in a positive direction.

2. Learn How to Communicate

We enjoy—and communicate best with—people who are just like us. When you meet someone with a style that is similar to your own, you tend to be approachable, open, and comfortable, resulting in increased understanding, increased appreciation, and a stronger relationship. If a person interacts (consciously or unconsciously) in a style that is opposite to yours, you will tend to shut that person out.

Since the words you say represent only 7 percent of your communication style and the ways in which you say those words represent 93 percent of your communication style, it is important that you pay attention to the messages you send.

What Is Your Political Style?

One of the most powerful senses you can develop is a sense of self-awareness. Why? Because if you know yourself and your style better than your colleagues know you, you are in a position of strength. If you know yourself and your style, and you understand your colleagues and their styles better than they do, you are in control.

To understand your own political inclinations and to understand the political culture in your organization, take the Political Tendencies Assessment (Exhibit 4-1), and find your style from the following choices. Then locate the styles of your colleagues, paying particular attention to the descriptors.

Exhibit 4-1
Political Tendencies Assessment

Use this assessment to measure your own political inclinations, and to identify the political tendencies of those you work with. Choose the statement that most closely describes you—and remember that there is no winner or loser and no right or wrong—there is only what is.

This may be difficult; you may think some of these do not apply at all. Just choose the one that is *most* like you.

1. Being perceived within my organization as "right" is
   A. Imperative
   B. Important only if everyone agrees that I'm right
   C. Important to me personally, but I'd never say so
   D. Important only if the facts prove I'm right

2. I have
   A. A forward-looking, aggressive, and competitive style
   B. A people-focused, consensus approach to decision making
   C. The ability to stay calm and controlled, even in chaos and turmoil
   D. The ability to do tough and complicated assignments right the first time

3. I judge people based on
   A. Their ability to get the job done quickly
   B. Their warmth, influential contacts, and commitment
   C. Their dependability and consistency
   D. Both the quality and the quantity of the work they do

4. I influence others by
   A. Competition, tenacity, and the strength of my character
   B. Interpersonal skills, charisma, confidence, and diplomacy
   C. Consistency, helping others, following through, and perseverance
   D. Facts, accuracy, data, attention to detail, and strategy

5. When I'm stressed, I
   A. Become impatient or demanding
   B. Become even more enthusiastic and optimistic
   C. Feel it on the inside, but don't show it on the outside
   D. Become critical (of myself and others)

6. My biggest fear at work is
   A. Losing control
   B. Not being liked
   C. The unknown
   D. High-risk decisions

Add your score:

_____ A

_____ B

_____ C

_____ D

Key: For this assessment, we will focus only on your core style, represented by the highest score.

More "A" answers: *The Senator*
More "B" answers: *The Communications Director*
More "C" answers: *The Press Secretary*
More "D" answers: *The Journalist*

If you are a *Senator*, your style may range from decisive and competitive to driving and demanding. In a political structure, your desire to win, be the first, be the best, lead, and challenge can come across as powerful—and sometimes as frightening to those around you. If you scored on the high end (5 or 6), be aware that you may have a reputation as a "political animal." A

Senator's verbal communication style is direct, commanding, specific, and to the point. Senators think fast, speak fast, maintain eye contact while speaking, have a strong handshake, and will be strong, clear, confident, and direct when communicating. Their written communications will be short, and sometimes bullet-pointed; Senators prefer short memos to lengthy letters (incoming and outgoing). Senators do not like verbose explanations: Get to the point when speaking to such a person.

If you are a *Communications Director*, the way your style is observed by others may range from social and trusting to shallow and superficial. In a political structure, the more recognition you have, the better—you love the spotlight. Getting recognition is your goal, and you gain acceptance and approval, develop and maintain relationships, and deliver results by influencing others. If you scored on the high end (5 or 6) here, be aware that you may have a reputation as a "political phony."

As a Communications Director, you are an emotional speaker, using expressive hand gestures, smiling, and personalizing your communications. You are energized, enthusiastic, persuasive, and friendly. You may use words like *fun*, *exciting*, or *recognition* in written communication, and you prefer written communication to the telephone. You may not listen very well, but, when you are listening, you have the ability to hear emotional tones in the conversation ("Stacy, you sound sad—is everything OK?").

If you are a *Press Secretary*, you speak slowly, in a thoughtful, relaxed manner. The way your style is observed may range from stable and steady to indifferent and apathetic. Typically good listeners, Press Secretaries will do just about anything for the good of the team—and, since they often keep their feelings of frustration and anger to themselves, they can sometimes feel like victims of a political structure that is swirling around them. If you scored on the high end (5 or 6), be aware that you may have a reputation as "politically oblivious."

Press Secretaries will not stand too close, and will often use small hand gestures with a speech pattern of warmth, calm, and steadiness. The Press Secretary will write clear, concise letters with excellent instructions or guidelines. A natural listener, the Press Secretary will try to hear and understand, will listen for ways to help the speaker, is most comfortable with harmony and sameness, is often resistant to change, and does not like to be rushed into decisions.

If you are a *Journalist*, you tend to ask questions rather than make statements, and you are slow and thoughtful in your speech, with limited hand gestures. The way your style is seen may range from accurate and systematic to perfectionist and critical. The Journalist likes to know and follow the rules, and where no rules exist, the Journalist makes them up. Journalistic style is alert and sensitive to what is going on around them, yet they are typically introverted, so they usually keep to themselves politically. If you scored on the high end (5 or 6), be aware that you may have a reputation as a "political dictator."

The Journalist is controlled, reflective, direct, and precise. Best with written data, the Journalist will always have facts in logical order. The Journalist's written communications will be precise and logical, with no room for error; as a listener, the Journalist will assess everything the speaker says. The Journalist's facial expressions will reveal nothing about his or her reactions, and he or she may discard *all* information provided by the speaker if *any* fact is incorrect.

Whether you are a Senator or a Press Secretary, a Communications Director or a Journalist, communicating effectively is a primary component of personal competence. Daniel Goleman, author of *Working with Emotional Intelligence*, summarized the skills of people with personal competence in communication this way:

1. Is effective in give-and-take, and in reading emotional cues in creating and sending outgoing messages

2. Deals with difficult issues candidly and quickly

3. Listens well, seeks common understanding, and welcomes the sharing of information completely

4. Promotes open communication and remains receptive to the bad news as well as the good news

An effective communicator—one who is personally competent in the skill—knows what he or she is feeling and why, and how it looks to others. An effective communicator works to understand others, and takes responsibility not only for what is said, but also for how it is said. As you become personally competent in communicating, you will understand the impact that your decisions and actions have on other people, and you will balance your own needs against that impact.

Understanding the styles and motivations of others takes practice and patience, but it pays off.

Art, a sales executive for a high-tech firm, had been calling on Jason, a potential client, for several weeks. Art and Jason had worked out every possible alternative and option for the Web solution Jason's company needed, yet Art could not get Jason to sign the contract to close the deal. When asked, Jason agreed that they had discussed all of the fine points, yet . . .

Art was anxious to get the contract signed for many reasons: This client represented a coup within his industry, the Web solutions they had created for Jason's organization were cutting-edge and fun, and, of course, there was the fact that this contract would be the largest ever signed for Art's company.

After coaching Art on style, we determined that Art was a blend of a Senator and a Communications Director—decisive, quick-thinking, social, influential, and optimistic.

We determined that Jason, on the other hand, was clearly a Press Secretary—wanting harmony, disliking change, and needing time to evaluate any risk.

Art decided to approach Jason from a "there is no risk here" position. He suggested that Jason take his time in considering the Web solutions they had worked out together. Within 48 hours, Jason contacted Art. The contract was signed, and Art's commission was over $1 million.

Take the time to identify—not judge!—your style and the styles of your coworkers. Watch for the signs, signals, words, and actions that show you who others are style-wise. When you understand your own style and the style of your coworkers, you can communicate with anyone about anything.

3. Be Honest

Honesty implies a refusal to lie or to deceive anyone in any way (including lying to yourself). When you are honest, you tell the whole truth in a constructive (positive, productive) way. No slamming, no digs or cracks, no gossip—only helpful and practical communication is allowed here.

How do you say it all while remaining truthful, positive, and productive? Most of us do not like to have conversations that will make us (or others) uncomfortable, yet there are some occasions in a politically charged environment when we need to have a talk that falls into the category of "difficult." There are ways to turn these fear-inducing, intimidating discussions into constructive conversations: focus.

- *Focus on the real issue.* Some people are so uncomfortable when receiving any form of feedback that they deflect the discussion from the issue at hand to some other issue—or, more often, some other person. Deflecting is a way to avoid responsibility and put you on the defensive; thus, the discussion becomes "about you" rather than "about the issue." Turn the discussion around and stay focused on the solution.

- *Focus on the behavior, not the person.* When you need to speak to someone about a difficult situation, do it gently. Focus on the person's behavior, not his or her personality. Make sure to take time to listen, and then move toward working on the desired outcome.

Try for an Oreo cookie: Present one positive feedback issue, one learning issue, then another positive feedback issue. Present each as a separate fact. Rather than saying, "Your report on the fraud audit was excellent, and you've done a great job of managing to your budget so far this year, but your team is filing incomplete credit reports on new clients, so you need to fix that," try this:

"We have three things to discuss. First, your report on the fraud audit was excellent—good job. Second, I've noticed that several of your staff have filed incomplete credit reports on new clients—when the credit reports are incomplete, the implementation date is delayed, it creates a challenge in accounting, and your employee's commissions are delayed. I'd like you to devise a plan to get that back on target and stay there, so that all of your credit reports are completed on time. Can you have the plan to me by next Monday? And finally, you are to be commended for managing to a very tight budget—congratulations."

Consider the following examples of feedback:

Good form for feedback:

- I like the general idea, but let's talk about this—here's the flaw as I see it . . .

- I certainly don't have a solution, but something isn't working for me about this idea. Let's work on this . . .

- Here's what I suggest that you consider . . .

Poor form for feedback:

- That idea sucks.

- That's not going to work.

- You don't know what you're doing.

You can maintain a sense of optimism in any difficult conversation by setting your focus on the future and being completely honest. Work on the solution.

4. Listen Up—Your Ears Will Not Get You in Trouble

Have you ever been on a phone call when you just "checked out"? The other person is talking, and you have missed the last, oh, 30 seconds of conversation. Then you are asked a question that you cannot answer because you have not been paying attention, and an unpleasant feeling washes over you. You missed the conversation because you were writing a mental shopping list, adding something else to your to-do list, answering an email, or just distracted by something that was more important to you.

Effective listening skills have a huge impact on how well we relate to peers, friends, and family members and how well we perform our work, yet we often take listening for granted. Great listening skills do not just happen—they have to be developed. Here are a few tips for becoming a better listener:

- *Do not interrupt.* If you are anxious to be seen as *right* and to have your views known, you may not allow others to communicate their thoughts completely (translation: you interrupt). A good way to stop yourself from interrupting others is to take notes—it will help you remember the thought to which you wanted to respond, help you interpret before you respond, and keep you from interrupting when you think you know the answer.

- *Be respectful.* When listening, keep in mind that everyone is a decision maker and customer for your ideas, so do not burn any bridges. Demonstrate that you are taking the other person seriously. Show respect for their point of view, even when you disagree.

- *Listen with open ears, warm eyes, and an open mind.* If you focus on what is being said without judging it, you will be able to use any valuable information or concepts. If you judge others while you are listening, your ears are closed.

- *Pay attention* not only to the content of what someone is saying, but also to the emotions the person is revealing (how the person feels about what is being discussed). If you find yourself reacting to others rather than responding, you may find that you are uncomfortable with their emotion, and the content goes right out the window. When you appreciate how people feel about an issue, your understanding of the issue will be deeper.

> *No one ever listened themselves out of a job.*
> *—Calvin Coolidge*

5. Is This the Hill You Want to Die On?

Activism is good. Misplaced activism is bad. Political battles in the office often gain strength like a hurricane: from outside forces. Consider whose battle you are joining, and whether you are jumping in because you want to be accepted or because the issue is important and values-based. When you understand your own motivation and the motivation of others, you will make better decisions about when to fight and when to move on.

6. Know Your Company's Objectives, and Contribute

As a takeoff from the "nose-to-the-grindstone" theory, do not take your eyes off the goals and objectives of your boss and your organization. Know the mission, vision, and purpose of your company and your unit, and view each political situation through the lens of corporate goals, rather than through the lens of power, domination, and needs. Use your strengths and skills to make a valuable, and visible, contribution.

7. Maintain a Sense of Humor (But Lose the Sarcasm)

Laughter is the very best medicine. Humor at work energizes our relationships, establishes trust, enhances communication, exercises our creativity, and reduces stress. Use your sense of humor to laugh at yourself and your predicament, to lighten a tough moment, or to solidify a team on a subject—but never at the expense of another.

Final Thoughts on Office Politics

Implying that you can "win" at office politics indicates that there is also a loser—and that is not the point of this process. Any time you work with human beings, you are subject to the complexities of various relationships: trust, credibility, communication, turf issues, and the multiple nuances of getting other people to do what you want them to, or to *not* do what you don't want them to. The focus, then, is how to leverage office politics as a form of personal influence, avoiding the possible hazard zones that can have negative consequences for you and your career.

Make listening well a major component of your strategy. Listen to the constructive criticism of others. Whether you agree with them or not, the opinions of your work and your style that others have can affect your career in a very real way. Listen, too, for clues as to which departments, projects, or skill sets are getting the most (or least) amount of attention (and funding). If you're in one of the areas that seem to be singled out as being more expensive or less effective than they should be, it is time to regroup.

Creating a strong political strategy is a method for getting a bigger return on your investment of time and energy, while enhancing your position at work. Let your strategy include collaboration, communication, and honesty; fight your own battles (and choose them carefully); keep your eyes on the prize; and keep laughing—proven ways to leverage workplace politics.

Concepts to Remember

1. Understand the distinction between
   - Collaboration and conflict
   - Collaboration and compromise
   - Collaboration and competition
   - Power and control
   - Power and strength

2. Avoid committing any of the Seven Deadly Sins of PLOP:
   - Persecuting or mistreating others
   - Gossip, rumor-mongering, or back stabbing
   - Personalizing events or the actions of others
   - Saying yes when you really mean no
   - Arrogance
   - Whining
   - Always needing to be right

3. Set boundaries around those who demonstrate the Seven Deadly Sins toward you.

4. Work to understand the style and motivation of others.

5. Practice communicating clearly—not just your inten-
    tions, but *how* what you say is received.

6. Practice integrity, always.

7. Always focus on the real issues, not on blame.

8. Focus, too, on *what* is best for the future.

9. When receiving feedback, listen and learn.

10. When delivering feedback, use the Oreo cookie
    approach.

11. Listen up:
    • Don't interrupt.
    • Always show respect (even when you disagree).
    • Pay attention to what is being said and how it is
      being said.

12. Know your boss's objectives and your company's objec-
    tives, and make a contribution.

13. Fight only your own battles, and choose them wisely.

14. Keep laughing—but lose the sarcasm.

5

Keys to Successful Workplace Relationships

Have you ever taken the time to watch the successful (and not-so-successful) people in your workplace? If you pay close attention, you will pick up the clues you need if you are to develop stronger workplace relationships for yourself. In a healthy corporate environment, you will find people who see problems as opportunities, demonstrate confidence (not arrogance), are loyal (not a doormat), are assertive (not hostile or stubborn), and are kind (but not weak). You will also notice people making and sharing observations (not judgments), thoughtfully responding to challenges (not reacting), and focusing on *what* is right (not *who* is right).

Problems or Opportunities?

One of the critical elements in developing healthy workplace relationships is redefining problems and challenges as opportunities.
If making the transformation from problem to opportunity is
not a natural process for you, the difficulty may be related to how
you view those problems: the distinction between disappointment and failure, your level of optimism, your opinion of
change, and your understanding of choice.

With the skill of transforming problems into opportunities,
you can develop successful relationships with practically anyone,
anywhere. The following information will help you to identify
the components you need to learn in order to exercise the ability to make the shift.

Disappointment or Failure

Disappointment is a part of life—not necessarily the fun part,
but a part nonetheless. Sometimes we experience disappointment
as a personal failure; therefore, we need to define the distinction
between failure and disappointment. *Failure* occurs when you
attempt a task and perform part of the process in a flawed way
(or omit an important part of the process). For instance, if I plan
to bring a product to market, but I do not understand the end
user, I will probably fail. It is a process thing, not a people thing.
A process failure can (and often does) open the door to regret—
the way in which we personalize the negative outcome, limiting
our ability to transform problems into opportunities.

Disappointment, on the other hand, occurs when an event
fails to meet our expectations or our hopes.

*Glenn is an executive in career transition—well regarded, emi-
nently qualified, well educated, and articulate. Glenn has been*

looking for a senior position for several months. He has used the direct mail approach in his job search campaign, sending résumés and cover letters to various executive recruiters and corporations across the country. He had hoped for a 50 percent return, and he experienced a 2 percent return (which is typical). He is feeling angry and disappointed because the process failed (he has not failed).

Ron and David were partners in a start-up. Friends for over 20 years, they created a solid business plan and marketing plan, and began building their high-tech business from the ground up. After 2 years of struggle, they began to sign clients, build a decent pipeline, and make money. Then David was offered a full-time position by one of the firm's new and prestigious clients, and he accepted, leaving Ron without a partner, without a friend, and without a major client. Neither of these men failed. There were integrity issues, yes; partnership issues, yes; disappointment, certainly. Failure, no.

Brian decided to accept a general manager position with a Fortune 500 company. Even though he had clues about the company's cultural and management issues, he was apprehensive about the trend of the country's economy, and he thought he had better snap up the job in front of him. Six months later, he knew that he had made a mistake: This was not the place for him. Scared? Yes. Disappointed? Yes. Failed? No.

If you are dealing with a problem and you are feeling disappointed, first reframe the problem as a temporary setback, rather than personalizing the event as a failure. If you can, consider the concept that disappointment is a good way to get you back on the right track—Glenn's job search, Ron's partnership, and Brian's career choices need to be reviewed from a strategic viewpoint, and each can be transformed into opportunities.

More on Optimism

Optimism, defined by Webster's as "an inclination to anticipate the best possible outcome," is a critical dimension in getting along and getting ahead in the workplace. Optimistic people expect the best for themselves, their projects, their partners, and their friends. Someone with an optimistic style understands that negative events in life are temporary—and external. Pessimism, on the other hand, can be defined as "an inclination to anticipate the least favorable or worst outcome for everything." Pessimists explain negative life events as permanent, internal, and outside of one's control (victim stuff).

While pessimists have a way of latching onto the worst possible cause for adversity (the permanent, pervasive, and personal), optimists latch onto the changeable, the specific, and the nonpersonal causes for any problem. When confronting any workplace problem, optimists have an edge—they head into the process of transforming problems into opportunities knowing that there will be a positive outcome. Pessimists, on the other hand, head into the process of transforming problems into opportunities with a strong belief that nothing good will come of their efforts.

Optimism is a learned behavior, and your level of optimism can be increased. Once you make the decision to shift your outlook for your future to ultimately positive, you open doors for opportunities you did not even know were there. If learning this skill sounds daunting, find a coach or therapist to work through it with you.

The C-Word: Change

Two caterpillars are enjoying another beautiful day, dining on the lush spring vegetation, when an exquisite butterfly floats by. One caterpillar turns to the other and says, "You'll never get me up on one of those butterfly things."

It is an unquestionable truth that life changes quickly and people change slowly. How you manage change is a choice: You can fight it, you can ignore it, you can work with it, or you can direct it—and whichever of these is your preference, change will happen anyway.

Some of us are natural change agents, variety-oriented and anxious to be a part of the brave new world. Some of us, however, prefer the comfort and security of sameness and predictability. Now more than ever, in this era of widespread change and uncertainty, success can be defined by how well we adapt to change. When we are the change agent, leading the charge, we feel that we are in control, and we adapt more easily. At other times, change is prescribed by others, sometimes disrupting the organization we have created in our lives—and if we feel that we have had little or no input into the change, we lose our sense of optimism for a positive outcome, and fear takes over.

Your resistance to change can be measured by what you have to lose or gain by changing, and your success is a result of knowing how to evaluate your resistance, identify your obstacles, plan for action, and do some fine-tuning. To improve your chances of working with change rather than resisting or merely surviving it, ask yourself these questions:

- What am I resisting?

- Have I experienced this feeling of resistance before, and if so, when?

- What control do I have over my response to this change?

- What control do I have over the outcome?

- What do I need to learn or know in order to make this change easier to accomplish?

- What responsibilities must I assume and what actions must I take now to assure a positive outcome?

Answering these questions will help you understand your change-aversion and help you determine what your next step should be. For Alison, a client whose company was in the middle of a merger, answering those questions was helpful in identifying exactly what it was she was resisting:

- *I am procrastinating on stack-ranking my employees for the merger and an impending layoff. I am resisting the possibility of letting people go.*

- *I have had this same feeling before—procrastinating when I am afraid of the outcome.*

- *I do have control over my response to the outcome. I can be sad or angry or happy.*

- *I don't have any control over the outcome, other than my input.*

- *I need to understand that whatever happens is what is best, and then I need to let that happen.*

> • *I need to get the review of my employees completed, present*
> *it to the merger team in a positive way, and trust that they*
> *will make the right decision.*

Alison was most uncomfortable with a potential negative change over which she had no control, yet her initial resistance to the change was only postponing the inevitable and tarnishing her reputation as a good manager. When she was able to realize what it was that bothered her, she was able to put it aside and to complete her work and her presentation without being tied to the outcome.

When turning problems into opportunities, you'll be faced with many forms of change—perhaps a change in your self-awareness, a change in your style, a change in an old, ineffective belief—but change will happen whether you wrestle with it or embrace it. The choice is yours.

> *Life is change; growth is optional. Choose wisely.*
> —*Karen Kaiser Clark*

The Other C-Word: Choice

We are constantly bombarded with choices—and opportunities. Sometimes we just do not like the choices we have.

We are what we think. If we choose to think that we are intelligent, successful, and happy, we are right. If we choose to think that we are never going to amount to much, never going to have a successful career, never going to have enough, we are right again. We can choose to approach our career—or our life—from the position of, "There will never be enough (so I must grab and push and struggle)." Alternatively, we can approach our career—and our life—from a position focusing on what we do have—which is more than enough—and strategize how best to use it. One operating platform is constrained by fear, and the other is liberated by gratitude.

Worry and Suffering, Another Choice

In my coaching practice, a recurring theme is often a sense of worry: "How will this turn out?" "Will my presentation be OK?" "What do they think of me?" Worry or concern over what may happen in the future will not change the outcome; it will, however, deplete your energy and your ability to think clearly. Worrying is a choice you make; suffering is optional.

In his book *Zen without Zen Masters*, Camden Benares writes of a young man who sought out a Zen master because of his constant worry and suffering.

> *"The man said that he had consulted one expert after another without success: "One person told me to give up sex and I did, but I still suffered. Another told me to give up meat and I did, but I still suffered. Another told me to give up sweets and I did, but I still suffered. I have tried everything that has been suggested, without success. You are my only hope. Please help me."*
> *The Zen master replied, "Give up suffering."*

Part of turning problems into opportunities is to recognize that you always (yes, *always*) have a choice. You can choose to be angry, you can choose to worry, or you can choose to be thoughtful and respond in a way that moves you forward. It is up to you.

> *If you think you can, or you think you can't, you're right.*
> —Henry Ford

Watch Your Assumptions and Beliefs

Webster's tells us that an assumption is a presumption, and a belief is a habit of the mind. Beliefs are actually assumptions that we have internalized—we make them true for us. Problems occur when we develop assumptions on the basis of limited or faulty information, or when we accept other people's assumptions as our truths—whether those assumptions are about a race, a gender, a culture, or a style. When we make assumptions without challenging the soundness of our thought processes, we are really just creating stories. When we create stories, we may react out of emotion, and this holds us all back.

For example, suppose a driver quickly parks in a spot you have been waiting for, hurriedly gets out of his car, and runs into the store. Your initial assumption is that this guy is rude and arrogant, and that he obviously thinks his time is much more precious than your time.

But what if that guy was in a hurry to get into the store because his wife had just been in an accident there and he wanted to ride with her in the ambulance? When we draw a conclusion about someone's behavior before we *know*, we are simply making up an ending based on an assumption.

Assumptions can be a good thing—when the stoplight turns yellow, you assume that it will soon turn red. Assumptions can also be barriers to successful workplace relationships if we simply assume that we know what someone is thinking, doing, or saying.

Be Aware of Your Fears and Judgments

Fear can also be a good thing, if you learn how to use your fear to move yourself forward. When your fears are needs based (I fear being wrong, I *need* to be right; I fear rejection, I *need* approval), you should deal with the fear by dealing with the need. Identify those needs and get them met forever, so that you can operate from a values-based system (see Chapter 1).

Stop Making Excuses

Another component of both taking control of your reputation and developing successful workplace relationships is to stop making excuses. When someone is making an excuse—for being late, for being wrong, for being human—it is always clear that this is what is being done—so why do we do it?

First, there is a distinction between an excuse and an explanation. An excuse is an attempt to absolve yourself of responsibility, to justify your position, and to remove blame. An explanation is an attempt to clarify without abdicating your responsibility.

- *Excuse:* "My alarm didn't go off."

- *Explanation:* "I didn't set my alarm properly and I overslept; I'm late, and I'm sorry."

One of these statements avoids responsibility; the other is fully accountable.

There are reasons why people make excuses. Perhaps you have unmet needs, and you choose to cover that up with this type of behavior. Maybe you are running on adrenaline and making too many promises that you just cannot keep. Maybe it is about putting up with "stuff" (mind clutter), or maybe you have not yet learned the benefits of integrity (translation: immaturity). Whatever the source of your behavior, find it, stop it, and build your reputation on integrity.

Perspective

A critical component of successful workplace relationships is awareness of your perspective. It's easy to say that we each have our own perspective on every issue under the sun, yet sometimes this perspective (anchored by our assumptions and beliefs) causes us to struggle, especially when we draw assumptions about others and what others are thinking.

I read an article on emotional styles that recounted this wonderful adage about perspective:

> To her lover, a beautiful woman is a delight; to a monk, she is a distraction, to a mosquito, a good meal.

So, what creates these differences of perspective? A lot of them come from what we have learned from our life experiences; some of them are made up (making assumptions)—and, according to Tara Bennett Goleman, author of *Emotional Alchemy*, the way we perceive (and react to) various situations depends on habits we don't even know we have.

When you are faced with a difficult situation at work, what is your perspective: Are you optimistic (the cup is half full), pessimistic (the cup is half empty), or toxic (what cup?)? The reason you respond the way you do involves your core beliefs about yourself. If you believe you will never get what you want, guess what: You never will.

Take the case of Lisa, Michelle, and Bob. Peers, each of these professionals held the title of director of operations for a real estate investment firm. Lisa was a "cup half full" person, Michelle a "cup half empty" person, and Bob a "what cup?" person. When their company announced a merger with Brand X, a larger organization, Lisa's immediate response was to contact her boss and ask how she could be part of the new regime. She wanted to know the initial direction of the merged companies, and how she could best position herself and her career within the new organization.

Michelle was quietly worried. She spoke with her peers in hushed, apprehensive tones, stating that she hoped she would still have a job when the dust settled. Her plan was to lie low and see what happened.

Bob was freaked out. He was certain that his job was going away, so he spent the next several days buffing up his résumé and making phone calls to recruiters with the aim of getting another job as quickly as possible.

All three of these people had an equal chance in the new organization, yet Lisa's perspective moved her forward, and the negative perspectives of both Michelle and Bob created barriers for their careers. Michelle did such a good job of waiting for the dust to settle that she was overlooked, and Bob had no confidence in the newly merged company or his potential career with it, and so made no attempt to hide his efforts to jump ship at the first opportunity. Lisa remained on board and was promoted to senior director, while Michelle and Bob were laid off—their jobs were given to two directors from Brand X who had shown confidence and trust in the future.

Identify the perspectives that are barriers to your successful workplace relationships, and the attitudes you demonstrate that may keep this year from being your best year ever. This can dramatically improve your career.

Distinctions to Remember

Confidence vs. arrogance: There is an *observable* difference between confidence and arrogance. Arrogance is self-important, inflated, and disrespectful. Confidence is quiet and strong.

Assertive vs. aggressive: To be assertive is to be self-assured and firm, and to be aggressive is to be forceful, antagonistic, and belligerent. Assertiveness is strength, while aggression is a weakness.

Loyal vs. doormat: To be loyal is to be a trustworthy, dedicated, and dependable employee, while being a doormat is to allow people to take advantage of you. One requires confidence, awareness, and strong standards and boundaries, while the other involves victim behavior.

Kind vs. weak: To be kind is to be aware of the feelings of others and to display compassion and concern for the well-being of others. Demonstrating kindness is not indicative of weakness—to be weak is to be vulnerable, helpless, and unproductive. Being *kind* is a strength; being *weak* is a limitation.

Observe vs. judge: Perhaps as a result of fear-based behavior, we attempt to fool ourselves into thinking that we are being observant when we are really being judgmental. When I notice that we are different in some way, I am observing. When I place a value on that difference, I have made a judgment. Judgments are like mirrors:

When I judge you on your actions or behavior, I am really trying to make myself feel better about how I behave in similar situations.

What vs. who: In your workplace relationships, do you want to be a respected equal, or do you want to be above everyone else? A respected equal understands the difference between *being* right and *what* is right. Someone who needs to be seen as superior may force his or her opinions on others in order to *be* right, while completely neglecting *what* is right. The need to be right is often based on an underlying need to control and to exercise power—a way to falsely inflate the self-image. If you feel compelled to interrupt and correct, or to notice and comment every time you see something that is not completely accurate, you are probably being driven by the need to be right or to make others wrong.

Respond vs. react: We spend a lot of our time reacting to the expectations and demands of others and their circumstances, rather than responding in a productive way. When you *react* to a bully's need to be controlling, an incompetent's need to be seen as capable, or a blamer's need to be right, your choices are limited: You can fight, avoid, surrender, or quit. When you *respond* to those types of behaviors, your choices are all positive and responsible; you maintain your equilibrium, your self-confidence, and your reputation.

Just One Second . . .

If your goal is to be a well respected, credible, trustworthy, and responsible person, it is time to shift away from negative behaviors. Identify any of the less effective behaviors that you demonstrate, and choose to apply more positive behaviors that move you forward. Catch yourself in the act of being arrogant, aggressive, critical, reactionary, or defensive, and follow this process:

1. Pause, take a deep breath, and ask yourself, "What is really happening here?"

2. Explore a little deeper—why are you behaving this way? What fear or need is at the source here?

3. Decide how you want this to turn out—what is the best action to take for your reputation, your career, and your life?

Use this three-step process to identify and shift other behaviors that are no longer effective. You will make better, well-informed choices for yourself.

Final Thoughts on Successful Workplace Relationships

1. Different individuals have different values, talents, beliefs, fears, and styles, each of which may have a substantial effect on the way the individual operates. We are all unique, and we are all valuable.

2. Acknowledge and appreciate your peers. Show support and appreciation for the work being done by others, and (sorry for sounding corny) you will receive much more in return.

3. Take responsibility for your actions—admit your mistakes, apologize, and move on. We are all human, and we all understand that mistakes happen, so when you are wrong, admit it and move ahead.

4. Understand that even successful workplace relationships are not perfect, and that you may have coworkers, bosses, and employees that you do not agree with, or just do not like. Learn from those experiences, maintain a keen awareness of what is going on around and inside of you, keep your reputation strong, and control your career.

5. Understand the distinction between
    • Disappointment and failure
    • Confidence and arrogance
    • Assertiveness and aggression
    • Being a loyal employee and being a doormat
    • Being kind and being weak
    • Observing and judging
    • Responding and reacting

6. Be aware of the connection between your fears and your judgments.

7. Fears can be needs based, so identify your needs and get them met—you will eliminate the fear.

8. Stop making excuses.

9. Managing change is a choice; change will happen, whether you fight it or embrace it.

10. Reframe your focus from *who* is right to *what* is right.

11. Give up worry and suffering—it never changes the outcome.

12. Be aware of your perspective: optimistic or pessimistic, narrow or wide, close or distant.

13. Choice: We are what we think.

14. Your assumptions about other people, especially about what they are thinking, are often wrong.

PART 2

GETTING AHEAD

Viktor Frankl (1905–1997) was an Austrian psychiatrist who was interned in a Nazi concentration camp, along with his wife and family, during World War II. His wife and family perished, yet he was able to emerge with a deep knowledge of human behavior and a theory that people's primary motivational force is the search for meaning. His life story has been an inspiration to many, and his book Man's Search for Meaning *has proved to be one of the 10 most influential books in America.*

Dr. Frankl's simple yet powerful theory of success and fulfillment is based on a simple drawing: On the success/failure continuum ..., success is defined largely by external measurements (your job title, the car you drive, the neighborhood in which you live, how much money you make, how you are per-

ceived by others). On the fulfillment/depression continuum, ful-
fillment is defined by internal measurements (how you feel
about what you have done, what you are doing, and what you
plan to do.) One can be absolutely successful and unfulfilled at
the same time; one can be a financial failure and thoroughly
fulfilled at the same time; one can be both wholly successful and
absolutely fulfilled at the same time.

		Fulfillment		
Failure				Success
		Depression		

Dr. Frankl's success/failure continuum

Applying Dr. Frankl's theory of success to getting ahead in our careers allows us to explore why we want to get ahead in the first place: Are we chasing success, or are we evolving our careers through personal growth? You can get ahead either way, but one path leaves you asking what is missing, while the other provides you with peace and strength and opportunities.

Soul Searching

When I was fully engaged in my corporate career, I woke up one morning and asked myself, "How did I get here?" The answer

110

was easy: It just happened. I had had no grand plan, no strategy; I had simply worked harder, faster, and longer than my peers, chasing success. Ultimately, I found myself in a job I didn't like, with a corporate culture that didn't match my values or strengths, and I didn't like the choices I made, the unhealthy relationships I developed, or *myself* while I worked there. I was living someone else's expectations for a great life, financially successful but personally unrewarding. At that time I did not know exactly what I wanted; I just knew it was not this.

Through coaching, I found that what I really wanted was a values-based life. I learned that achieving both professional success and personal fulfillment was an attainable goal, and I wanted my work, my friends, and my life to be oriented around my values. To get clear on how to fill the gap between where I was and where I wanted to be, I had to recognize a few things:

1. That I was *good* at some work processes that I did not enjoy (for instance, cold calling on sales prospects)

2. That I was *marginally good* at some work processes that I really liked (for instance, consultative selling)

3. That I was *really good* at other work processes that I really liked (gap analysis, problem identification and resolution, coaching)

Bingo—values meet skills. And, I found that as a pathway to dealing with all of the components of getting ahead, knowing your values, your strengths, and what you *like* make the entire process easier.

Ask yourself:

1. Do I know the difference between what I am good at and what I enjoy?

2. Do I know the difference between being driven by needs and adrenaline and being motivated?

3. Do I know the difference between my own values and priorities and the values and priorities of my organization?

Once you have identified those critical areas—the differences between what you like and what you are good at, between needs-driven behavior and self-motivation, and between your values and those of your organization—you can work on filling the gaps, because that is the road to success and fulfillment for you.

A good coach can help you work through those questions to identify what will bring you success and fulfillment. My clients have added the following components as important elements of their own success and fulfillment:

- Imagination, to envision what is possible

- Setting, and reaching, high goals

- Loving what you do (blurring the line between work and play)

- A readiness to take smart risks (and a willingness to fail)

- Surrounding yourself with diverse, competent people (and helping those people to learn and grow)

- Integrity, always

- Balance, to keep everything in perspective

Life Balance

Years ago, discussing life-balance issues with an employer—taking time for family, for personal growth, for fun—was an invitation to be terminated. When I was in my twenties, I was raising two children, going to school, and working full-time. I was promoted into a mid-management job, and my boss told me, "Don't ever tell me you can't make it to work because of your kids. This job is your first priority." Of course, it was not long before I demonstrated that my first priority was different from what he thought it should be, and my job went away.

Today, though, most employers embrace the theory of life balance—that employees are happier and more productive when all of the components of their lives are in balance. Finding your life balance is a fundamental component of success, fulfillment, and ultimately getting ahead (and living to enjoy it). Several years ago, Brian Dyson, vice chairman and COO of Coca-Cola Enterprises, shared his perspective on life balance during a commencement address:

> Imagine life as a game in which you are juggling some five balls in the air. You name them—work, family, health, friends, spirit, and you are keeping all of these in the air. You will soon understand that work is a rubber ball. If you drop it, it will bounce back. But the other four balls—family, health, friends, and spirit are made of glass. If you drop one of these, they will

be irrevocably scuffed, marked, nicked, damaged, or even shattered. They will never be the same. You must understand that and strive for balance in your life.

Finding and maintaining that balance in your life is one of the most important strategies you can use when moving ahead in your career, because a balanced life is based on your values, and you make smarter choices when you respond out of your values, rather than reacting from your needs.

The following chapters will show you how to create a balanced life while evolving your career by tapping into your strengths, skills, and values. Whether you are dealing with management-level office politics, trying to create visibility without appearing egotistical or boastful, or coaching your boss to be a great leader, the focus will be on advancement through personal development and balance.

As Dr. Frankl demonstrated to the world during his lifetime, there is another reason for achieving professional success and personal fulfillment: People who are both successful and fulfilled make the world a nicer place in which to live. They build their reputation on integrity, accomplishment, and honesty; shift problems to opportunities; change what they can (and accept what they cannot change); share credit; take responsibility; and show respect. In the face of the challenges of getting ahead in the workplace, it is not always easy to do the right thing, but it is always worthwhile.

6

Vision, Mission, Goals

[Alice] was a little startled by seeing the Cheshire Cat sitting on a bough of a tree a few yards off. . . .

She went on, "Would you tell me, please, which way I ought to walk from here?"

"That depends a good deal on where you want to get to," said the Cat.

"I don't much care where—" said Alice.

"Then it doesn't matter which way you walk," said the Cat.

—Lewis Carroll, Alice's Adventures in Wonderland

Before you can genuinely focus on getting ahead, you have to consider where you want to go. If you are motivated to shine at work, you have a clear vision for your career and your life, with clear-cut goals, and you are emotionally intelligent enough to accept accountability for your actions, then you will deliver results that will propel your career forward.

It Starts with a Vision

Yogi Berra's advice, "If you don't know where you're going, you might wind up someplace else," is well taken. Before you can deliver stellar results, you have to have a vision for your future, a mission for your actions, and meaningful goals—otherwise, you just might wind up "someplace else."

Creating a personal vision statement and a mission statement and defining the goals that support them is one of the most powerful steps you can take in advancing your career and your life, as it involves identifying your most important roles, what you want to do, and how you want to do it. Creating a vision statement and a mission statement for your team is another powerful way to identify what is most important and what has to be done, by whom, and when. Whether for your team or for yourself, a vision statement and a mission statement become your compass and a significant source of guidance during an ever-changing, fast-paced life, allowing you to keep your eyes on the target so that you can deliver exceptional results.

The terms *vision statement* and *mission statement* are often used interchangeably, and when organizations do not "walk the talk," these terms may seem completely without substance. For clarity, then,

- Your vision is what your eyes see as possible for your career and your life.

- Your mission is what your hands will do to manifest your vision.

Vision: What You See as Possible

Your vision is your dream—without editing—for your future. A personal vision will include what you see as possible for your career and your life—where you want to be. Your vision should be easily understood so that you can easily transfer it into your mission statement, and then into individual goals.

To develop a vision statement, I ask my clients to complete the following process.

What Do You Value?   In Chapter 1, we examined personal values. Refer to your Values Worksheet, and focus on those things that are most important to you. These words are powerful motivators that influence your choices, habits, and lifestyles. Sharon, a marketing executive and coaching client, found that the following were her top values:

- Communication

- Creating

- Making a contribution

- Leading others

- Giving

- Accomplishing

Review the values you identified in Chapter 1, and list your top six values.

What Are Your Strengths and Talents?   Everyone has strengths and talents that enable him or her to do certain things and to make a contribution at work and in life. Consider your strengths and talents—they can be technical skills, behavioral skills, or both. These may be skills that others recognize in you or strengths and skills that others do not see. Sharon, the marketing executive, reviewed her work history, and created her list of strengths and talents based on both the things that she felt were significant and compliments that she had received from others:

- Can influence others

- Organized

- Independent

- Disagrees diplomatically

- Excels in troubleshooting

- Works well on a team

- Is self-directed

- Has a sense of urgency

- Negotiates solutions well

- Has a great sense of humor

- Effectively communicates authority

- Enjoys variety

Review your work history and the compliments you've received. List at least six strengths and talents.

What Is in Your Way?   Just as you have strengths and talents that enable you to do certain things, you may have habits or behavioral styles that prevent you from getting what you want in your life and your career. These may just be skills you have not learned yet; you may be aware that you are disorganized, or easily ruffled, or easily angered. List no more than three such habits that might prevent you from realizing your goals.

Sharon reread a few of her performance evaluations from past years to identify her barriers:

- Can snap at people when she's busy

- May be thinking of her response while the other person is still speaking

- May overextend—tries to accomplish too much in too little time

How Do You Want to Be Remembered?   How would you like people to think of you when you are gone? What words would your closest friends, colleagues, and relatives use to describe their thoughts and feelings about you? Sharon, the marketing executive, found this question easier to answer by writing her own epitaph:

People say that I always had a sense of independence, a mind of my own, a great sense of humor—that I was a great communicator, an excellent planner, with patience, courage, and optimism, and with a very level head. My workmates say that

I was fun and interesting to work with, that I was creative and generous with my time and ideas. They say that I always had an opinion, yet I was able to share that opinion in a way that brought people together, and that I enjoyed finding solutions to problems that others didn't even realize existed. They say that I made some good decisions and some bad ones, and that some of my relationship choices left me on the verge, yet I rebounded, and I became an even stronger, wiser, and kinder person. They say that I gave lots of love and devotion in close friendships, laughed a lot, and even learned to listen better as I got older.

Refer to Exhibit 6-1, and select up to three words that you would like your friends and loved ones to use to describe you (or use your own descriptors). If you choose to write your epitaph, underline or highlight the words that you find to be the most appealing descriptors of you. From her epitaph, Sharon chose the words *courage*, *patience*, and *generous*.

Exhibit 6-1
Descriptors

__ Accountable	__ Grateful
__ Ambitious	__ Hard-working
__ Amusing	__ Influential
__ Balanced	__ Insightful
__ Caring	__ Loyal
__ Committed	__ Organized
__ Compassionate	__ Optimistic
__ Courageous	__ Patient
__ Creative	__ Philanthropic
__ Dependable	__ Principle-centered
__ Educated	__ Proactive

__ Enthusiastic	__ Respectful
__ Ethical	__ Responsible
__ Fair	__ Self-reliant
__ Faithful	__ Sensible
__ Forgiving	__ Truthful
__ Fun	__ Trustworthy
__ Giving	__ Understanding

Vision Statement

Sharon's vision statement became

To develop professional success and personal fulfillment in my life, I will:

Lead *a life centered on my values of communication, creating, making a contribution, leading others, giving, and accomplishing.*

Appreciate *my strengths and talents, and be known as a person who is influential, independent, diplomatic, and a great problem solver; works well on a team; negotiates solutions well; has a great sense of humor; and enjoys variety.*

Be honest *with myself by acknowledging that I can be irritable, may not listen well, and may overpromise, and by constantly striving to learn and grow to shift my barriers into strengths.*

Envision *myself becoming a person who is courageous, patient, and generous.*

Advance *my career by leading a values-based life, appreciating and using my skills and talents, and learning to identify and overcome barriers; by achieving balance between my work and my personal life; by creating and maintaining a highly visible and superior reputation for excellence at work;*

*by helping my team to become even better at what they do,
individually and as a team; by asking for input and feedback
from others; by setting higher standards for my behavior; and
by earning a promotion to senior vice president of marketing
by June 1.*

Now you are ready to prepare your vision statement. Complete the statements in Exhibit 6-2 from the lists you have created. This statement can become the foundation for your solid personal vision statement. Complete it, add to it, print it, frame it, *read* it—let it be a dynamic reminder of what you see as possible for your life.

Exhibit 6-2
Vision Statement

Complete the statements below from the lists you created earlier in the chapter.

To develop professional success and personal fulfillment in my life, I will:

Lead a life centered around my values of: (list your values here)

_____   _____

_____   _____

_____   _____

Appreciate my strengths and talents, and be known as a person who is: (list your strengths and talents here)

_____   _____

_____   _____

_____   _____

Be honest with myself by acknowledging that I can be: (list barriers here)

_____   _____

_____   _____

_____   _____

and by constantly striving to learn and grow to shift my barriers into strengths.

Envision myself becoming a person who is: (list your descriptor words here)

_____   _____

_____   _____

_____   _____

Advance my career by leading a values-based life, appreciating and using my skills and talents, learning to identify and overcome barriers, and achieving

_____

_____.

Mission: What You Will Do, Specifically, to Make Your Vision a Reality

Your mission statement will provide commitments to the actions you plan to take to ensure that your vision materializes. The following principles are necessary for a successful and complete mission statement:

- *Reserve:* When you create your strategy, you must plan for more than you need. Expect the unexpected—plan what it will take to meet the goals required to realize your vision, and then add 50 percent more than you think you will need for a reserve. For example, assume that your vision for your career states that you will become the top sales producer in your company. To do that, your mission statement indicates that you will close one sale per week. If six calls are required to generate one appointment, and three appointments are required to close one sale, then your action steps will include making a minimum of 18 calls per week. To develop a reserve, make 27 calls each week for insurance, increasing your potential from 1 sale per week to 1.5 sales per week.

- *Resources:* It will be essential for you to have the necessary resources available, including people, places, or things that you may not have needed in the past. To achieve your goals, it may be necessary for you to expand your network. As you build your strategy, consider what resources you may need, and plan how and when you will get them. Review your current network and resources to see if there is more that you can do with what you already have.

- *Actions:* It is critical that you know what actions you need to take in order to move forward and that you know that the actions you take are consistent with your goals and your vision.

- *Support:* Use mentors, bosses, friends, or a coach to assist you in reaching your goals and realizing your vision. The more people you involve in your goals, the better. There may be times when you do not need additional support, but you will know that it is there when you need it.

Since your mission statement is directly connected to your vision, it must be motivating, and it must indicate specific steps that you will take to make it happen. Sharon completed her mission statement in this way:

Sharon's Mission Statement: In order to realize my Vision, I will do the following:
Habits to create:

- **Monthly**: I will assess my career, my client relationships, and my budget. I will meet one-on-one with team members, and create a strategy to assist them to be successful. I will review my personal time, my relationships, and my personal finances to stay on track.

- **Weekly**: I will keep track of how I spend my time. I will document my promises to others. I will network with at least one peer-level employee each week.

- **Daily**: I will create a reserve of time, energy, and resources. I will review each day's completed actions and plan for tomorrow's actions before I leave the office for the day.

Skills to learn:

- I will learn to organize my time, learn to say no to time-wasters, and learn to mentor my employees.

Behaviors to shift:

- I will listen well.

- I will take a deep breath before speaking, even when I'm busy.

- I will provide healthy feedback to my employees.

- I will stay balanced in my career and my personal life.

Support structures to create:

- I will find and work with a mentor within the office to help me see how to grow and improve.

- I will ask my family to let me know if they feel that I'm not paying attention to them.

- I will ask for feedback from my team, my clients, and my internal customers as a way to improve.

Finalize your own mission statement by completing Exhibit 6-3.

Goals

Now you can take your mission statement and turn it into specific goals. Set your goals so that they are just out of your immediate reach (to make them interesting, challenging, and fun), but not out of your control or unattainable.

Exhibit 6-3
Your Mission Statement

Your mission will be formed by completing this sentence:
In order to realize my vision, I will do the following:

Habits to create:

Monthly _____

Weekly _____

Daily _____

Skills to learn:

_____

_____

_____

Behaviors to shift:

_____

_____

_____

Support structures to create:

_____

_____

_____

Sharon's Goal Worksheet

GOAL # 1: *Promotion to Senior Vice President*

1. What Value Does this Goal Honor? *Leading others, making a contribution, accomplishing*

2. What are the benefits to me, both personally and professionally of accomplishing this goal? *Career advancement, increased visibility, increased variety, increased salary and benefits*

3. What resources do I need to accomplish this goal?

Equipment/Technology/Education

HAVE:	NEED:
Degree in communications	MBA
Knowledge of sales, marketing, business development	Knowledge of other departments and divisions
Allies in Sales, Biz Dev	Allies in Operations, Accounting, HR

4. What help, assistance, or collaboration do I need?

People or Resources

HAVE:	NEED:
External Coach	Internal Mentor–Sales?
Basic understanding of job function	Job description–HR?

	Rebuild relationship with Richard (Accounting)
	Better visibility with CEO, COO, and Board

5. Am I willing to do whatever it takes to reach this goal? *Yes, I am!*

6. Make your Plan:

What individual tasks must be completed, and by when?

#	Task	Due Date
1.	Get job description from HR, get application and interview process information (panel?)	3/24
2.	Analyze need for/benefits of MBA	3/30
3.	Schedule peer-level lunch/coffee/breakfast	Ongoing one per week
4.	Schedule mentor meeting	3/27
5.	Call Richard in Accounting, rebuild	3/24
6.	Work on Visibility Plan with Coach	4/2
7.	Schedule meetings with CEO and COO	4/5
8.	Research and prepare for interview process: questions that will be asked, questions I should ask	4/15
9.	Submit application, participate in interview process	5/1

Choose at least three goals from your vision and mission statements, and complete a Goal Worksheet on each (see Exhibit 6-4). When you have completed a worksheet for each goal, make a calendar listing when you will achieve each goal and when you will carry out *each activity* required to achieve the goal. If you find yourself procrastinating, review your worksheet to uncover your barriers (usually the only one keeping you from reaching your goals is you).

Exhibit 6-4
Goal Worksheet
GOAL # ___ **GOAL NAME** _____

1. What value does this goal honor?
   _____

2. What are the benefits to me, both personally and professionally, of accomplishing this goal?
   _____
   _____

3. What resources do I need to accomplish this goal?
   _____
   _____

Equipment/Technology/Education

HAVE:	NEED:

HAVE:	NEED:

4. What help, assistance, or collaboration do I need?

People or Resources

HAVE:	NEED:

5. Am I willing to do whatever it takes to reach this goal?

_____

6. Make your plan:
   In priority order, what individual tasks must be completed, and by when?

#	TASK	DUE DATE

#	TASK	DUE DATE

Optimism, Again

You are what you think. To be successful in your career and fulfilled in your life, you must strike a balance between the goals you want to achieve and your opinion of your chance for success. If you *think* you can . . .

Final Words on Vision, Mission, and Goals

Goal setting without a vision can leave you working to achieve someone else's expectations. A vision without action is just a daydream.

Working with a vision and a mission, and identifying the goals associated with them, is a powerful tool that you can use to benefit every area of your life. This process allows you to know exactly what you want to achieve, and how to get it; and setting appropriate goals allows you to know what you have to concentrate on and improve in order to enjoy your career and live a life you love.

People who set goals for themselves make better decisions, they are more organized, they have greater self-confidence, they feel more fulfilled, and they are more enthusiastic. Developing your vision and your mission gives you an empowering long-term strategy, and setting meaningful goals gives you short-term motivation. Make this process a priority for your career and your life.

Concepts to Remember

1. Before you can deliver stellar results, you have to define meaningful goals.

2. Before you can define meaningful goals, you need to create your vision statement (what you see as possible for your future) and your mission statement (what you will do to achieve your vision).

3. Tie your vision, your mission, and your goals to your values, skills, and strengths.

4. Find and use the resources and support that you need in order to reach your goals and realize your vision.

5. Build a reserve into each goal—plan for more than you think you will really need.

6. Take action to make it happen.

7

Management-Level
Office Politics

*It is good to recognize when political games are being played,
but that doesn't mean you should join in. If you want to play
games, pick a sport.*
          —Gina Dias, Corporate Controller, NVT, Inc.

The trouble with the game of management-level office politics
is that it is not at all like a game. There are no rules, no referees,
no time-outs—only winners and losers.

This version of office politics is cultural, a style of communication and evaluation that is used by and in organizations.
Office politics at the management level is different from peer-
level office politics. It is much less "junior high school" and much
more serious—the stakes are higher, and recovery from a political blunder may be difficult or impossible. Political maneuver-

ing is much more pronounced in the senior ranks, where much of the manager's performance evaluation is based on subjective measures rather than tangible results; therefore, the participants in management-level politics typically focus only on the professional success end of the success/fulfillment grid.

In my corporate days, I moved up through the ranks to management by *playing the game*. At first I did not play it well: I showed support for unpopular subordinates who I thought had potential for growth; I spoke up when I disagreed with opinions, assumptions, or initiatives; and I refused to follow the "in crowd" in their padding of expense reports (passed on to clients). My behavior was the political equivalent of running with scissors.

Then I decided to "play," and play I did. I dressed like them, talked like them, shunned those people who were on the "outside," and cavorted with those people who were "in"; I always agreed with the "right" people, and I voiced my objections or concerns only to people who "didn't matter." And I could not stand myself.

This was the point in my career when I realized that I just could not be this way. I did not want to be a cruel, gossipy (albeit well-dressed) political conspirator, and then go home to my 10-year-old son and teach him about kindness and integrity. Something had to change.

During my early days of coaching, I identified and came to understand my own personal values, and I realized just how different my values were from those espoused by my then-employer. I also woke up to the theory of *personal needs* and realized that I had attempted to participate in the political mumbo-jumbo in order to be accepted as part of the group. When I really *got* the idea that management-level office politics was all about *power*, I could see that my peers and I were simply jockeying for position in a nasty political arena. Then I was able to let it go.

It's about Power, Silly

With mergers, acquisitions, downsizing, and corporate compression, there are even fewer spots available for advancement; office politics is about power, and the competition is fierce. Some career experts offer advice on how to become politically powerful by generating fear in others, complete with instructions on fear-inducing topics to discuss at meetings, what type of eyeglasses to wear, what type of clothing to buy, what desk accessories to display, and what fountain pen to use when signing letters. Remember the 1980s? This type of power was popular then and continues to be popular in some circles today, and it is that greed-power-win orientation that has resulted in a series of giant corporate implosions. The CEOs of these organizations had reputations for blasting through whatever—or whoever—was in the way: They had power. They have experienced financial success at the expense of others, but their personal fulfillment is difficult to ascertain in the chaos of criminal investigations.

There are at least three choices that you can make in a politically charged management culture:

1. You can choose to capitulate and become one of the Machiavellian power-hungry (at what expense needs to be determined by you—my experience with this style was not comfortable for me, or for anyone who knew me!).

2. You can choose to hide and do your best to stay under the radar. (Doing nothing is a choice—not a life-fulfilling choice, but a choice nonetheless.)

3. You can choose to operate from a platform of integrity, shifting the focus to ethical leadership or authentic power. (This choice changed my life.)

Authentic Power

If you shift your focus from trying to generate fear and manipulate the current political-power system to creating and maintaining a leadership culture based on an ethical foundation, then you will be responsible for finding effective, pragmatic solutions to problems, while demonstrating trust, commitment, and values that are shared with those who are led. Ethical leaders are responsible for creating a culture that moves the company and all of its employees forward—and in which politicking is no longer required.

From the two action options given earlier, choose the brand of power you will use—politicized power or ethical leadership—not on the basis of what is currently going on in your workplace, but more appropriately on the basis of who you are and what you want. By defining success for yourself, your life, and your career, by becoming aware of the culture and style of the organization in which you wish to evolve, by identifying the political structures that are being displayed and those who are displaying them, and by making some smart choices, you can be both professionally successful and personally fulfilled.

Shifting to Ethical Leadership

Every work situation on the planet exposes you to the complexities of human relationships, including trust, credibility, communication, conflict, influence, and motivation (yours and theirs). How you as a senior manager handle problems, influence people, and deal with the pace of your environment and with the rules and procedures set by others is only one element of your style, political tendencies, and cultural fit. You must also understand how other people use *their* style.

In the following examples, we will investigate the four basic styles—dominant, influential, steady, and conforming—from both the Machiavellian power player (MPP) and the authentic power (AP) perspectives. You will notice that while both may have the same basic style (drawn from Marston's work, referred to in Chapter 3), the difference is in how they leverage what they have. Read the description of each style, and use the strategies listed to leverage what you have in your situation.

The Dominant Style   If you work with or for a decisive, ambitious, and pioneering individual, you are dealing with someone with a dominant style. These people love to lead; they want authority and results (from themselves and from those who report to them). They treasure freedom from control, supervision, and details. They love variety: new programs, projects, and ideas.

- *MPP:* As the need for power and authority overrides the value of collaboration, people with this style can appear abrasive, pushy, demanding, quick to anger, impatient, and egocentric.

- *AP:* When a desire to deliver results supersedes any need for power, people with this style are more likely to appear determined, inquisitive, fast-paced, results-oriented, and responsible.

If You Are Dealing with an Individual Exhibiting the Dominant Style   Remember that both the MPP and the AP with this style are motivated by others who verbalize assertively, display energetic effort, provide direct answers, accept feedback, seek new challenges, and work independently. What is different between the MPP and AP is the way in which each generates and responds to support and followership: The needs-driven behavior of the MPP will appear demanding, fear-inducing, and win/lose, whereas the values-based behavior of the AP will appear encouraging, motivating, and win/win.

Tips for Dealing with an Individual with a Dominant Style

1. Stick to business; be clear, specific, and to the point. Don't waste the person's time by wandering off the point or engaging in idle chitchat.

2. Provide opportunities for a win/win situation; don't back someone with a dominant style into a corner.

3. Whenever possible, prepare your case well in advance of speaking with a person with a dominant style. Avoid speculation; keep your support material or backup documentation handy, but use them only when asked.

4. Always present your case to someone with a dominant style in logical order—gaping loopholes, fuzzy logic, and disorganization will probably generate a negative reaction.

5. When you disagree with someone with a dominant style, clearly convey that you are taking issue with the facts, not with the person.

6. Set boundaries for yourself, and be prepared to enforce them. An MPP can easily go into intimidation mode and become abrasive and pushy, so be prepared to redirect those efforts by enforcing your strong boundaries.

Refer to Chapter 2 for a review of setting and enforcing boundaries.

If You Exhibit MPP Tendencies in the Dominant Style, Try the Following Tips

1. *Calmness.* Waiting patiently is not a normal behavior for a highly dominant, highly political individual. To exercise patience, you must choose to be composed (rather than agitated), to show kindness (despite having to wait), and to recognize that other people's time and effort are equally as important as yours.

2. *Empathy.* Understanding, compassion, and apologies are not easily offered by a highly dominant, highly political individual. To shift into a more empathetic style, first engage your self-awareness skills: Notice the effect of your style (abrupt, negative, or irritated) on others. Then offer an explanation and an apology: "I'm sorry, I was much more abrupt than I had intended—let me rephrase." The belief you must hold in order for this to be authentic is that people respect, appreciate, and are loyal to those who acknowledge the impact of their words and actions, whereas people fear and distrust those who demand.

3. *Enjoyment.* A highly dominant, highly political person can miss life's best pleasures because he or she does not know how to relax. Taking pleasure in life by relaxing—and celebrating—is an integral part of personal fulfillment. In an effort to push ahead, MPPs may not only ignore their own successes, but disregard the successes

of the team as well. If you have just finished a huge project, put your feet up and feel the relief, or create a way to celebrate your win. When a colleague or subordinate reaches a milestone, take the time to acknowledge it and celebrate with that person. Enjoying a sense of satisfaction provides renewal so that you can move ahead, and creates an environment of motivation for others.

4. Try shifting out of politics and into ethical leadership by showing understanding, listening to others without interruption, increasing your followership skills (allowing you to become one of the group rather than over and above), and accepting responsibility and accountability for your words and actions.

The Influential Style   Highly influential people want popularity and social recognition. What makes these folks shine is any opportunity to be creative. Experiencing variety, having the freedom to speak, and having plenty of people to associate with are hallmarks of someone with an influential style. If you are looking for detail orientation, you have come to the wrong place. These are strategists with big-picture ideas.

- *MPP:* As the need for social recognition becomes paramount, a political influencer can appear overenthusiastic, superficial, and often forceful in her or his attempts to get you to go along with her or his way of thinking.

- *AP:* With personal needs taken care of, people with this style are more likely to appear persuasive, inspirational, magnetic, trusting, and trustworthy.

If You Are Dealing with an Individual Exhibiting the Influential Style   Remember that both the MPP and the AP with this style are motivated by others who openly express their opinions, demonstrate good-natured optimism, project personal warmth, appear poised and self-confident, and willingly cooperate and collaborate. The MPP will be more self-promoting (possibly taking credit for others' successes), overextended (but rarely taking responsibility for missed deadlines), and driven by a need to be liked. The AP will leverage his or her natural tendencies toward interaction and socializing with healthy, realistic optimism, checking first to understand others, then to be understood, and working to draw out alternative perspectives when making decisions. Where an MPP may make multiple, often unrealistic, commitments as a way of gaining support and approval, APs make only commitments that they know they can keep.

Tips for Dealing with an Individual with an Influential Style

1. Allow time to break the ice; don't be abrupt or impersonal.

2. Ask for the person's opinion and discuss goals; don't drive too hard on facts or tasks.

3. Plan to discuss actions that support the person's goals and intentions; don't stifle her or his contributions.

4. Keep your interaction fast-moving and fun, and provide ideas for implementing action; don't waste time.

5. Put details of your discussions in writing; don't leave decisions up in the air.

If You Exhibit MPP Tendencies in the Influential Style, Try the Following Tips

1. *Sincerity.* Be direct in relating your concerns to others, and use a no-nonsense approach. Avoid overpromising or making too many commitments, overinflating the seriousness (or the triviality) of any issue, or using convincing, cajoling, or seducing methods to get people to see things your way. Speak genuinely; how you say it is more important than what you say.

2. *Purpose-filled.* Insist that work be judged by high standards, not by the popularity of the worker. Identify an accepted standard of operation, and use it—published, objective standards are a strong foundation for goal development and a basis for evaluating others in an unbiased and principled way.

3. *Trust.* When people are working with or for someone who appears superficial in his or her style, that style negates any sense of trust. If you overpromise and underdeliver or if you operate from an unrealistically optimistic platform, you will not be seen as dependable, reliable, truthful, or inspiring. Work to meet your time obligations by underpromising and overdelivering. Be authentic when providing critiques of events and ideas, using facts as a basis for disagreements.

4. Try shifting to the ethical side of the influential style by doing what is right, rather than focusing on being seen as the good guy. Be accountable, assume responsibility for yourself and your work, and follow through. Pay

attention to the details, meet the demands of others with clear, concise answers, and use common sense—apply your no-nonsense, practical approach to delivering results.

The Steady Style   Individuals with this style want security. If change is required, they want plenty of time to adjust to it. They stick with tradition and the status quo (the way things have always been done) when working on projects and processes and in their relationships, both at work and at home.

- *MPP:* Because of a natural aversion to change, people with this style often avoid the struggle for power. When they do, though, you may see passive-aggressive tendencies (saying yes and meaning no), with a fundamental resistance to anything different, outwardly masked by apathy. Since the biggest fear is not being appreciated, the political player with this style may seem duplicitous as he or she attempts to balance the need to be accommodating with the desire for stability.

- *AP:* With needs and ego issues out of the way, leaders with this style will appear relaxed, patient, and steady, with a sincere appreciation of people and processes, an understanding of change (still allowing for time to process the change), and great listening, calming, and planning skills.

If You Are Dealing with an Individual Exhibiting the Steady Style   Remember that both the MPP and the AP with this style will be motivated by others who stick to their convictions and are conscientious, principled, and persistent. An MPP will appear aloof and apathetic, resistant to change, and suspicious, while an AP will encourage others in an effort to gain cooperation, work to accept necessary change, and stay in balance (and control), even under pressure.

Tips for Dealing with an Individual with a Steady Style

1. Use an icebreaker to open your discussion; show your genuine interest in the person as a person; don't rush too quickly into business or into your agenda.

2. Be patient, draw out the person's ideas, and listen carefully. Don't force the person to offer a fast response to your ideas, and don't interrupt the person when he or she is speaking.

3. Provide appropriate assurances; don't promise something that you cannot deliver.

4. Watch and listen for what's just under the surface, and ask questions; don't mistake the person's willingness to follow as an indication of satisfaction or agreement.

5. If a decision is required, allow the person time to process (think). Don't force a quick decision.

If You Exhibit MPP Tendencies in the Steady Style, Try the Following Tips

1. *Say no.* This is a basic decisiveness issue. Learn how to say no in order to give yourself more control over your life and your career. Try refusing an invitation with

firmness and grace. Try declining a request to take on additional work without feeling guilty. Saying no does not make you any less accommodating; it does make you more responsible and in control.

2. *Spontaneity.* Being intense and focused is admirable, until it runs your life. Being carefree is an art—you want to learn how to let go in a safe setting by taking an opportunity to say what you feel. To make this work, you have to let your self-censor take a vacation so that you can promote your relaxed and unstructured side.

3. *Delegate.* It is hard to entrust important work to someone who may not complete the task in the same manner you would—especially when it would take less time to do it yourself. The problem is, though, that failing to delegate work (all the way to micromanaging) creates distrust in good employees, while allowing mediocre employees to just show up and get a paycheck without taking any responsibility for learning and delivering results. Again tied to a need to be accommodating, for people with this style, the fear of not meeting specific requirements is second only to the fear of the unknown. Change your mantra to "efforts are to be shared equally," and commit to the care of others what is often expected of you.

4. Try shifting to the ethical side of this style by demonstrating your independence, individuality, inventiveness, determination, objectivity, self-satisfaction, self-directedness, and courage.

The Conforming Style   Individuals with this style want to know that they are doing a good job and doing things right. They are drawn to policies and procedures, and will follow those that have been established (or create them when none exist). They work well alone, have high expectations for themselves and others, are incredibly organized and analytical, and are self-competitive.

- *MPP:* Because of their "Lone Ranger" approach, people with this style are rarely seen in the highly charged political arena. When they are at the upper levels, though, their need to comply with authority may override the value they place on quality, security, or accuracy, and you may see people with this style become overly critical (minimizing those who respond emotionally), dependent on standard operating procedures, and perfectionist, putting others on the defensive.

- *AP:* With a sense of balance, people with this style will set high standards for themselves and subordinates, yet allow for learning (mistakes) and growth. They will demonstrate conscientiousness, weigh their actions against stated goals, provide order, and assume an investigative role when problem solving, proving their spirit of experimentation.

If You Are Dealing with an Individual Exhibiting the Conforming Style   Remember that people with this style are motivated by others who maintain a direct course of action, are practical about costs and operations, offer meaningful facts, demonstrate clear, concise reasoning, and have an ability to plan well. While the MPP will relate to others in an evasive, critical, and worrisome way, an AP will respond in a diplomatic, tactful, open-minded way.

Tips for Dealing with an Individual with a Conforming Style

1. Provide people with this style with sufficient information and time to enable them to process the decision they need to make. Don't try to convince them or "sell" them on your idea.

2. If you disagree with them, use data, facts, and testimonials from respected people. Don't fall back on personal opinion or feelings as evidence.

3. Prepare your case in advance, and be linear in your presentation; don't be too personal or informal.

4. Use an "action plan," scheduling dates and objectives. Don't overpromise results; err on the side of conservatism.

If You Exhibit MPP Tendencies in the Conforming Style, Try the Following Tips

1. *Self-esteem.* People with this style tend to be overly critical of themselves and others, indicating a self-esteem deficiency. Try building your self-esteem and self-respect by doing the following:
   • Identify your personal qualities, that is, those things about you, the skills you have learned, and the skills you are developing. Focus on your potential and your values.

- Change to positive self-talk (how you think about and talk to yourself). Stop condemning your faults—change what you can, and leverage what you cannot change.
- Don't try to measure your value by using someone else's yardstick. Self-esteem is home grown.
- Focus on your accomplishments; congratulate yourself on achievements, whether large or small. Each day, remind yourself of the things you do well, and of the courage you have shown.
- Establish realistic goals, and learn from failure. If you have setbacks, allow yourself to become a problem solver.
- Visualize success. Mentally rehearse succeeding in everything you do before you do it.

2. *Feedback.* Take criticism in stride—do not take it personally, and do not strike back. Keep your eye on the goal of quality, and seek out constructive suggestions. Make your daily affirmation one of "personal toughness is directed sensitivity."

3. *Analysis paralysis.* Move from planning to doing—act on the facts that you have, and prepare to alter your course if and when new information appears. Moderate caution is wise; excessive caution wears down your confidence by preventing you from having the opportunity to learn by doing.

4. Try shifting to the ethical side of this style by questioning the rules; by being candid, yet respectful; by being less of a perfectionist; by being more respectful

of others' efforts, ideas, and beliefs; and by being collaborative.

Staying Out of Hot Water

Now that you know yourself and the political behaviors in your current work environment, it is time to learn how to avoid the negative consequences associated with the dangerous side of the power-hungry. The first step is to recognize that at the senior level, your job focus changes from largely internal to partly or mostly external. As you speak to outside groups, vendors, or clients at the senior levels, your interpersonal skills will be equally as important as your presentation skills and your ability to interact effectively with the political structures of other companies and organizations. As you build the trust of your employer and your colleagues, you will also build the trust of external executives.

Another thing for ethical leaders to focus on is generating a decision-making process, especially at the senior levels, that is more collegial than independent. While this helps to avoid surprises, it is also an opportunity to build in collaboration, responsibility, and accountability. Remember, too, as we saw in *The Godfather*, "Never go against the family in public"—that is, never contradict your boss, your company, or corporate initiatives in a public setting. If you disagree with a decision or an initiative, the place to discuss it is within your offices, not in public. If the decision with which you disagree is illegal or immoral, review your standards, boundaries, and values, and deal with it. If the decision represents an operational or practical difference of opinion, however, discuss it inside and support it outside. If you are unable to do this, you are in the wrong job.

Final Thoughts on Management-Level Office Politics

We know that our careers will probably change several times during our adult lives (unlike our parents, whose careers were typically a one-stop event). We also know that in order to be valuable to our current and future employers, we need to keep up with what is going on both inside and outside of our current employment situation, operationally and politically.

I have read that between the years 1800 and 1900, it took 100 years for the world's body of knowledge to double. By 1940, the world's body of knowledge was doubling every 20 years. By 1970, it was doubling every 7 years. Today, the world's body of knowledge doubles every 2 years. It is estimated that by 2015, the world's body of knowledge will double every 35 days. Think about that: all of the knowledge of all of humanity doubling every 35 days.

I have found the best way to handle office politics is to focus on values and on becoming a "knowledge broker," and this is my recommendation to my clients. As you climb the ladder of corporate success and wade through the myriad political styles, one of the key assets you can trade is your knowledge.

Once you have decided to be a knowledge broker, you have made a commitment to being a lifelong learner. Then, it is a matter of being aware of (and researching) opportunities to learn, both inside and outside of your office. The payoff is obvious: You will have all of the knowledge of all of humanity available to you. You will also experience a universal truth: Learning is much more fun than knowing.

In a never-ending chase for success, some people choose the low road (I tried it myself), while others honor their standards, boundaries, and values—the high road (much more attractive). This is a choice you can make, and if you find yourself in an organization that does not respect your style of ethical leadership, it may be time to look for another assignment. I did just that, and I have developed incredible professional success and personal fulfillment beyond my wildest vision—working in a job I love, with people I love, without any inkling of office politics. And you can, too.

Concepts to Remember

1. Understand management-level office politics for what it is: power.

2. Observe and understand the distinctions between the MPP and AP styles, and choose your standards and boundaries accordingly.

3. Practice ethical leadership and followership.

4. Identify your own behavior style, and leverage it.

5. Identify the styles of your colleagues and your management, and work to communicate in a style that honors who you are, while respecting who they are.

6. Build your self-esteem.

8

Creating Visibility

Julia Turner sat at the counter of Schwab's Drugstore on Sunset Boulevard in Hollywood. As she sipped her soda, the 15-year-old beauty did not notice William Wilkerson, publisher of the Hollywood Reporter, *watching her every move. He walked up and introduced himself to the young woman, and a star was born: Julia was discovered and transformed into the film goddess known as Lana Turner.*

Now, *that* is visibility—you put yourself in the right place at the right time, and you are whisked off to fame and glory (or so the legend goes).

There are a couple of things wrong with this story. First, that meeting took place at the Top Hat Café in Los Angeles (not Schwab's), and second, it's no longer 1935. The waiting-to-be-discovered approach does not work in this century; if you want to move ahead, you have to create a strategy for becoming visible.

Under the Radar

Many people still believe that the nose-to-the-grindstone approach will reap its own rewards. It will not. What will reap continued rewards is creating and projecting an accurate, positive image of yourself in order to get people to know and recognize you, your strengths, and your potential. If you feel like you are flying under the radar, you may find yourself bypassed for important assignments or missing out on positive performance evaluations, salary increases, or promotions that you deserve. The trick is to design a visibility strategy while avoiding the impression of being self-serving, self-promoting, or grandstanding.

The Hitch in Your Gittalong

If you want to create a positive image and a high level of visibility for yourself in your workplace, you want this image to be real, and you want to be ego-free, you are going to have to review your values and your needs (see Chapter 1). You will also have to develop three fundamental behaviors:

1. *Self-confidence.* This is an inner belief that you will succeed. This capacity is not genetic, it is behavioral and experiential—a blending of your natural optimistic/pessimistic tendencies with how well (or not so well) you have done in the past. If your self-confidence is low, try the suggestions in Chapter 7 on building your self-

esteem, or consider working with a coach or therapist to rebuild your self-confidence, as this is a critical part of your career advancement.

2. *Overcoming fear.* There are countless types of fears, and many of them show up at work. While we may not see people running and hiding under their desks, we do see fear showing up in the form of isolation, arrogance, hostility, and other ineffective behaviors. The Four Fatal Fears that keep us from being our happiest and best were described by Larry Wilson and Hersch Wilson (authors of *Play to Win!*) as

   • Fear of failure (so I'd better not take any risks)
   • Fear of being wrong (so I'd better always be right)
   • Fear of rejection (so I'd better not speak up)
   • Fear of being emotionally uncomfortable (so I'd better not try anything new)

   Developing a visibility plan and putting it into place will engage all of these fears in some people, and some of these fears in others. These fears are often an overextension of needs (especially under stress).

3. *Taking risks.* Creating visibility requires you to take smart risks, and often. Demonstrating a willingness to take calculated risks is often cited as an example of the skills required by the new knowledge worker, one that is necessary for continued improvements in service and productivity, as well as for your visibility plan. How much of a risk taker are you? Take the quiz in Exhibit 8-1, and read the scoring key that follows to interpret your results.

Exhibit 8-1
Risky Business: Are You a Risk Taker?

Respond to all of the statements using the following scale:
1 point: Doesn't sound like me at all.
2 points: Sounds like me some to most of the time.
3 points: This is me.

____ I am known in my office as the person with new and unusual ideas.

____ I often create new and inventive solutions to old, stale problems.

____ My motto is: Do something, even if it's wrong.

____ At work, I have made more than one expensive mistake during the last year.

____ I never miss an opportunity; I'm willing to try just about anything.

____ I am vocal in meetings, and I share my ideas with my manager, his manager, and everyone else all the way up the ladder.

____ I have made recommendations and heard the word *no* at least once during the last month.

____ My boss gives me all the space and information I need to try new things and create new solutions—there's no fear here.

____ Total score

Scoring Key

8–13: Risk-averse. If you scored in this range, it will be important for you to determine whether your cautious tendencies are based on the cultural standard at your workplace or on a personal inclination to avoid the unknown. If risk taking is not respected in your work environment, you are not likely to take many risks; it may be time to consider taking yourself to a more risk-rewarding organization. If taking risks is not a comfortable and natural process for you, work to identify and deal with whatever is keeping you stuck (perfectionism, fear, analysis paralysis).

14–19: Risk-aware. You are ready to rumble. You have the ability to evaluate the chances you take before you leap, and you are willing to fail occasionally in an effort to find new ideas and solutions.

20–24: Risk-extreme. You are definitely a risk taker, but be careful that you are not branded as reckless or irresponsible. Balance your desire to be the best, lead the field, or be the winner with consideration of the opportunities and threats you may encounter—*before* you jump.

Growth or Fear?

These three important prerequisites to creating positive visibility involve one simple process: To build self-esteem, overcome fear, and begin to take smart risks, you must first choose growth over fear. This is a conscious choice that you make—you acknowledge the doubt or fear, understand your reference point for the doubt or fear, and make a decision based on what is best and right, rather than on the doubt or fear.

With renewed self-confidence, having made the decision to choose growth over fear, and being determined to take smart risks, you are ready for the next step.

Shameless Self-promotion

In straightforward terms, shameless self-promotion is simply marketing—the process of knowing what you have, identifying what people want, and then letting them know that you have it. Self-marketing, shameless self-promotion, and creating visibility are the same thing—in order to deliver what is wanted, you need to know yourself, know your market, develop a plan, and be persistent.

If we were talking about any other product or service, you would probably be quite comfortable jumping in and trying a new marketing approach. For some, however, the concept of self-marketing sounds more like a series of ego-based tactics designed to convince, seduce, manipulate, or pressure someone into something that he or she just does not want. Not so.

Self-Marketing Plan Development

Self-marketing is a systems approach to success that will help you become a more effective communicator, time manager, leader, and team player. The system of self-marketing helps you establish, direct, and coordinate your marketing efforts. Preparing a self-marketing plan forces you to assess what is going on in your industry and your organization, and how those goings-on affect your business, your team, and your career. Developing and using a self-marketing plan also provides a benchmark for later measurement.

Work through the following process to develop your self-marketing plan:

1. *Key qualifications.* Write a clear and objective assessment of who you are—your strengths, skills, and values. Also identify your gaps.

- Where are you in your career, and where do you want to be?
- Is your reputation stellar or secret?
- Is your productivity exceptional or imaginary?
- Are your technical skills up-to-date or out-of-date?
- Are you the "go to guy" or the "who is that guy"?

Review your past performance evaluations, and identify your growth pattern and your avoidance pattern. If there is a common "improve this" thread in your past performance, make a point of learning that skill first.

2. *Organizational needs analysis.* Consider the following:
   - What is the corporate mission, what are the short-term and long-term corporate goals, and how does your work currently affect the bottom line?
   - What are the internal or external challenges or obstacles that your company will face in the next 6 months? In the next year?
   - How can you help your organization move forward toward its goals, given your current level of expertise?
   - Who is your target audience?

3. *Potential liabilities.* Taking into consideration your organizational needs analysis, your key qualifications, and your gap analysis,
   - What are your potential liabilities? These could be real or perceived—what do you believe are barriers to your moving ahead in your career? List four possible issues.
     a. Leverage those issues. List your strategy for dealing with each potential liability, using some

of the recommendations given throughout Part
1 and at the end of this chapter. Be real, honest,
and proactive by identifying your potential
hazard zones early and managing them. If you
have trouble seeing these zones, work with your
mentor or coach to make sure you get them out
of your way.

4. *Objective statement.* Based on your research so far, state
   your career objectives. Be specific. Your objectives
   should be clear and measurable, and should have a time
   line for achievement.
   - Make sure your objectives are consistent and not in
     conflict with one another.
   - Be sure that all of your actions support your
     objectives.

   Setting your objectives and finalizing the remaining components of your marketing plan will also serve
   as a reality check: Do you have the resources necessary
   to accomplish your objectives?

5. *Strategy and implementation.* Write out what you will
   do, and when. Make sure that the strategies you employ
   to increase your visibility are in line with your own values (not based on your needs) and support your objectives. (See the recommended visibility strategies in the
   next section.)

6. *Measure the impact.* Make a checklist of your action
   items, and keep track of how many of those strategies
   you employ (or how often you employ them). Check
   in with yourself regularly to evaluate the effectiveness

of your visibility campaign, and check in with your mentor or coach to keep it real.

Fourteen Strategies to Create Visibility

If you are honoring your values and playing to your strengths, you are also working to do what you love. The following strategy recommendations will help you comfortably gain recognition inside your office, regardless of your starting point.

1. *Get organized.* Create a file that contains your résumé, letters of acknowledgment or thanks from internal and external clients, your performance appraisals, and notes of classes or seminars you have taken. Create a special financial section, including pay stubs, benefits statements, and information on comparable salaries in your field. (See Chapter 15 for suggested online sites to research this information.)

2. *Keep track.* Use your daily planner, electronic or on paper, to keep track of what you have accomplished each day. You will be able to review your productivity and accomplishments daily and weekly, and you will have a clear record for your next performance review (or to update your résumé).

3. *Read.* What journals or magazines does your boss read that you do not? What other publications are available in your field? Find at least one new source of information, read it, and discuss it with your boss.

4. *Make your boss your biggest fan.* Since your manager's success is tied to your success, work with your manager to understand how your work affects his or her goals, then work to meet and exceed those goals. Do not be shy here, either: Ask your manager to help publicize your successes.

5. *Contribute to the meeting agenda.* Add a topic to the team meeting agenda, and prepare to speak about it. You could plan to share information on a project or idea you have been working on, or to gather information for a future project or initiative. In either case, you will need only a few minutes to make a big impact and get people to see you and your ideas.

6. *Write a project update report.* Do not wait to be asked; when you have progress to recount, write an unsolicited update. There is no need to be boastful; this update can be sent to your boss and to appropriate peers or colleagues as a short, accurate description of your progress and next steps. Then follow up!

7. *Develop allies.* This internal version of networking can include developing relationships with people in other departments or asking a more senior person to be your mentor.

8. *Observe role models.* Watch what others do to gain visibility in an ethical, productive way. Watching the visibility strategies used by others (and their avoidance behavior) will give you a sense of what works and what

does not. You will also be able to assess what creative tactics are most comfortable for you.

9. *Help others be noticed.* This is based on the theory of abundance rather than scarcity. Here is how it works: When you focus on what you lack ("I need the visibility; he doesn't"), you create an atmosphere of not having enough (scarcity), but when you focus on what you have ("Your good work is making us all look good"), you will actually end up with more (abundance). When you help others to get noticed, you will find that those people will help you in return. Try noticing someone doing a good job, and tell that person so. See how practicing abundance has its own rewards.

10. *Volunteer for task force and committee work.* A great way to be seen, and to stay on top of new initiatives, is to volunteer to participate in planning sessions or meetings for social or work-related events.

Moving On Up

In your plan to move up to the executive level, you will have to create a positive image outside of your office as well as inside.

1. *Join an outside professional organization.* Go to conferences; speak up in discussions; have people notice your ideas. Choose your venue carefully; emphasize those groups where you are likely to meet people from different levels in your industry. Join a group whose charter and work is valued by your employer, and use the connections you make and the information you learn

to let people know of your work with that group: "At the Commonwealth Club meeting last night, we discussed hosting an Economic Trends Summit. I'm collecting names of volunteers who would like to work on the planning committee." You are instantly seen as an informed, informal representative of your company, and that translates into leadership.

2. *Write articles.* Trade magazines, company newsletters, and local newspapers appreciate timely, original essays, articles, and letters to the editor. Most trade magazines (and other magazines and newspapers) have a "writer's guidelines" section on their web site directed toward people who are interested in submitting articles—some even have recommendations for future articles. Write an article about your industry, your area of expertise, or a recent experience; once it is published, send it or information on where it appeared to appropriate and interested people in your target audience.

3. *Arrange for speaking engagements.* Look for organizations that accept outside speakers—networking meetings, trade shows, and local chapters of larger organizations appreciate articulate and informed outside speakers.

4. *Apply for board membership or do committee work for nonprofits.* This is another way to gain outside exposure, develop new relationships with people outside of your current organization, and exercise additional leadership skills. Use the Internet to search for organizations that need your talent on their board or on a specialized committee within a board.

Seven Secrets of Self-Marketing

There is a delicate balance when it comes to shameless self-promotion, and you do not want to be guilty of overkill. When used appropriately, a personal marketing campaign will open doors and help you advance in your career. The seven secrets given here are key factors in making your visibility plan work seamlessly.

1. *Make commitments and keep those commitments.* The quickest way to lose credibility is to make promises that you do not keep. If you are drawn to make commitments in an effort to please others, but then find that you cannot keep those commitments, remedy the situation at once. Tell your colleague or boss that you have overbooked your calendar, and that you will have to extend your delivery date (but do not simply ignore the initial commitment date). In the future, *under*promise; that is, if you think you can complete a task or project by Wednesday, tell your boss that you will have it to her or him by Friday. Then, if you do deliver by Wednesday, or even Thursday, you will look like a hero.

2. *Demonstrate reliability, honesty, and respect.* These three behaviors are inseparable, and they are all required as part of creating a positive self-marketing plan. You cannot fake these behaviors—either you practice them or you do not, and if you do not, you need to get a coach to help you move them up on your priority list.
   - *Reliability.* Like being trustworthy, being reliable is a quality that merits confidence or trust. If you walk the talk, if people know that you deliver on

your promises, if you keep your word, you are
known to be reliable.

- *Honesty.* This is a measurement of the decency of
  your character—your refusal to lie, steal, or deceive
  in any way. Honesty includes honor, suggesting
  high personal standards, and a high regard for the
  standards of your profession, calling, or position.
- *Respect.* To treat someone with respect—as you
  would be treated—is simply to create and
  demonstrate strong personal standards.

3. *Employ initiative and optimism.* This includes a readiness to seize opportunities or to convert problems into
   opportunities, to pursue goals beyond expectations, to
   influence others, and to operate from a platform of
   abundance and hope for success, rather than a fear of
   failure. People with this skill know how and when to
   take the initiative to solve problems and develop new
   ideas that will improve operations.

4. *Show a sincere appreciation for your internal and external clients.* This is not a place to be superficial. Take the
   time and effort to notice your clients' good work, and
   share your appreciation with them. Every time you
   speak to one of your clients, listen to that client carefully, and come up with one thing to appreciate.

5. *Look for opportunities to send the message that you are
   hard at work.* This applies to everyone, but more specifically to remote workers. Without becoming a victim
   or a martyr, make sure that the people who should
   know that you are working do know it. Use the strategies here to share your productivity and progress:

- Be available. If you work from home, let your boss, your team, and your internal and external customers know the specific times when you will be available during the day to field calls. If you have a regular at-home work schedule, send an email update on changes in your schedule to those who should know about your work. If you are based at home, but travel for work, set similar guidelines for your availability, sending more frequent "Where's Linda" emails—short and to the point.

- Whether you are an in-house or a remote employee, let your boss, your team, and your customers know your standards for responding to telephone calls, email, and other correspondence, and stick to it.

- If you have joined your company as an off-site employee, you haven't been exposed to your company's culture, so you miss the opportunity to know what is customary and acceptable in terms of customer service and work style. Ask to spend time in the office—for training, for meetings, or to participate in brainstorming.

- To avoid becoming "out of sight, out of mind," join as many staff meetings as you can, even if you attend by phone or computer. Ask to participate in on-site meetings with the in-house staff whenever possible, and use this precious "face time" in the office effectively—arrange to see the people who are most important to your career.

6. *Exhibit professionalism.* This involves the elements of your conduct—your standards and boundaries—that establish you as being ethical, courteous, conscientious,

and respectful in your workplace. When you create visibility for yourself, this is what people see first. If you cannot be described as being professional in your workplace, work with your mentor or coach to shift into a more professional style.

7. *Use attraction.* The theory of attraction is summed up by one sentence from the movie *Field of Dreams:* "If you build it, they will come." Creating visibility in your career can be Zen-like. And while that may sound contradictory to all of the information on the previous pages, consider this: You will not be convincing anyone, selling to anyone, or chasing after success. Using the theory of attraction, you *draw* what you want toward you like a magnet.

For example, I facilitate several executive networking meetings throughout California each month. The purpose of these meetings is to allow executives and professionals to get together, share contacts, develop relationships, and maintain a sense of connection with others outside of their own organizations—especially when they are in a career transition.

As a coach, I could easily transform this into a solicitation of coaching clients, but I do not. While I share with the participants what it is that I do, I simply offer myself as a resource for information, contacts, options, and solutions (free). All the participants know that they can contact me anytime, and that I will do my best to connect them to the person, web site, or information that they need. They also know where to go when they want to hire a good coach—and many of them do. I never solicit, I *attract*.

This same attraction theory will work for you in creating visibility. Without cajoling, convincing, seducing, or politicking, you can attract people to you by being aware of your audience, by generously sharing knowledge, by authentically supporting others, and by getting your own barriers (needs) out of your way.

Final Thoughts on Creating Visibility through Self-Marketing

It is true that being visible, enjoying (and leveraging) attention, and voicing your opinion on your industry, company, team, and community are part of life in the senior ranks. If you want to be a participant in your own career rather than an observer of it, if you want to take control rather than waiting to be seen, then you will need to face old fears and take new risks. Some strategies will feel right and some may feel awkward, but you need to start taking action to move ahead.

Concepts to Remember

1. Practice shameless self-promotion.

2. Create a positive (and accurate) visibility plan for your career.

3. Know what you fear and why, then make a choice on how you want to deal with it.

4. Understand your own risk aversion and make it work for you.

5. Work on your self-confidence.

6. Get organized.

7. Keep track of your accomplishments.

8. Read, learn, and grow.

9. Speak up at meetings.

10. Write a meaningful, unsolicited report.

11. Develop allies in other departments.

12. Observe role models, and learn.

13. Help others with their visibility.

14. Volunteer for committees and task forces at work.

15. Join outside professional or industry groups, and participate in committee work.

16. Write articles.

17. Arrange for speaking engagements with groups that are interested in what you know.

18. Become a board member of a for-profit or not-for-profit organization.

19. Make commitments and keep those commitments.

20. Be reliable, honest, respectful, optimistic, professional, and resourceful.

21. Use attraction.

9

Coaching Your Manager

Ben, the senior vice president of sales for a financial services organization, was in the process of recruiting a replacement for the regional VP covering business development and sales in the Eastern Region. This senior position required a professional with expertise in consultative selling, sales development, account management and expansion, client service, and staff management, and budget and P&L accountability in the $20 million range.

While the selection process was going on, Ben's boss, Ryan, told Ben to consider Ryan's 23-year-old, just-graduated daughter, Sally, for the open regional VP position. Ben reviewed Sally's résumé and realized that this would be her first professional job; while she had been a great student and had received a bachelor's degree in liberal arts, she had no business develop-

ment experience, no account management experience, no client service experience, no staff management experience, no budget experience, no P&L experience—and no financial services experience either.

By the time Ben contacted me as a coach to help him work through this dilemma, he had already given the problem a great deal of thought. If he responded to Ryan's request in the negative, he was in danger of insulting his boss (by rejecting the boss's daughter), being directed to hire the young woman anyway, or both. If he hired the woman, she would require an enormous amount of Ben's time for training and direction; other than sales clerk in a trendy clothing store, Sally had no workplace experience.

Ben decided that the best way to deal with this problem was to use a coaching approach. Even though Sally would not have been included in the interview process had Ryan not insisted that she be considered, Ben scheduled Sally to participate in the process, along with three other candidates. Standard procedure when hiring a regional VP was to conduct a full day of interviews, first with Ben, then with the regional VP's peers, and then with the client service team. When the interviews with all candidates had been completed, Ben returned to Ryan for a discussion.

"I think that your daughter is bright, enthusiastic, and articulate," he said. "While she is not as experienced or as qualified as the three other candidates I have interviewed, I think she may be able to grow into the job. Clearly, though, it will take a lot of help and assistance from her peers and from me. Let me make sure I understand why you think she should be considered for this particular job. What do you want for your daughter in this role?"

Ryan said, "I want my daughter to have a head start in a solid company, I want her to be successful, and of course I want to help her in any way I can."

"Well, since we are unable to reduce the requirements of the job for your daughter," Ben said, "she will be held account-able for producing the same results as anyone else who held the job, even if that person has had several years of experience. Will this be fair to her and help her become successful?

"Another point to consider," Ben said, "is that no matter how hard we try to avoid it, and regardless of how hard she works or her results, every time she walks into a team meeting, a company meeting, or a client meeting, people will look at her and say, 'She has this job because she is Ryan's daughter.' How can we make sure that she is evaluated as objectively as her peers are, yet has an opportunity to build a reputation of excellence on her own? If she is offered this VP position, are we cheating her of success based on her own merit?"

It did not take long for Ryan to see the potential disaster this appointment would have created. He wanted to help his daughter, but if he forced her into a job for which she was patently unqualified, he was virtually ensuring her failure. Sally's name was removed from the selection process; the decision to eliminate her was Ryan's. After this discussion, Ben's relationship with Ryan was stronger than ever, because Ryan knew that Ben was loyal and honest, and that together they had come to the right conclusion.

The Coaching Process

Your relationship with your boss may have more to do with your success and advancement in your career than just about any other factor. Whether you are in a new job or a remote job, or you have been in your position for months, knowing how to coach your boss will improve your career and your life.

The process of coaching is simple: You check your ego at the door, and you work out what is best. Coaching *up* is just a process of working with your boss to obtain the best possible results for your boss, your organization, and you. You do this by honoring and respecting each other's ideas and intelligence through dialogue and brainstorming, without pushing a personal agenda, instructing, or demanding that others see things your way. Coaching is not political maneuvering; rather, it is a deliberate effort to bring understanding and cooperation into a relationship between individuals who often have different perspectives. Think of your role as a coach (whether you're coaching up, down, or sideways) as a process of understanding what organizations want from their people, what leaders want from their teams, and what employees want from their leaders.

As a prerequisite to developing your coaching style, while you must continue to focus on delivering results, you must also know your own motivations, values, and needs (refer to Chapter 1 for clarification). These motivations (perhaps to make a contribution, to enjoy yourself, to learn, to earn respect, to make friends, to feel trusted, to work with people you trust and admire, to be part of a team, to share your talents, and to be valued) are absent of ego and are your springboard for coaching and helping others, even your boss.

Are You—and Your Boss—Coachable?

To be able to enter into any coaching relationship, you need to be coachable yourself. Take the Coachability Quiz (Exhibit 9-1) to determine your coachability, then reread the questions with your boss in mind (better still, have your boss take the quiz, too). Then look at the scoring key.

Exhibit 9-1
Coachability Quiz

Circle the number that comes closest to representing how true the statement is for you, then add your total score and consult the Scoring Key.

Consider these statements, and answer honestly:

Less True/More True	*Statement*
1 2 3 4 5	I am open to learning.
1 2 3 4 5	I am willing to be influenced.
1 2 3 4 5	I readily reveal my thinking.
1 2 3 4 5	I am ready to "try on" new concepts and ideas.
1 2 3 4 5	I identify, and explain, my assumptions.
1 2 3 4 5	I encourage others to explore my ideas (or assumptions).
1 2 3 4 5	I listen to others, giving them time to fully express their ideas.
1 2 3 4 5	I seek to understand the views and ideas of others.
1 2 3 4 5	When responding to another's view, I ask, "What led you to that viewpoint"?
1 2 3 4 5	I am someone who can share my success with my boss.
_____	**Total Score**

> ### *Scoring Key*
>
> **10–20:** If you scored between 10 and 20, you probably are not coachable at this point. Review the statements on which you scored a 1 or 2, and learn what you must do to upgrade those behaviors and skills for yourself. Refer to Chapters 1 and 2 for needs, values, standards, and boundaries work.
>
> **21–40:** You are coachable, but you need to pay special attention to your standards and boundaries, listen carefully to others, and avoid defensiveness.
>
> **41–50:** You are very coachable. Make sure that you and your boss demand a lot from each other.

Coaching Guidelines

Now that you know your own coachability status and you have at least a sense of the coachability status of your boss, let's move on to three important guidelines for coaching *up*:

1. Lead, Follow, Coach Great organizations rely not only on dynamic leaders, but also on dynamic followers, and both can be great coaches. Leadership skills are often touted as the main factor in getting ahead, yet when you are on a *team*, you must also have followership skills. But what are followership skills?

Followership skills are those that allow you to move together with others along a set path. This does not imply that you are unqualified for or incapable of leadership; it means that you can work with and for a leader, toward a goal, with others for a cause. Followership skills include

- Receiving and accepting ideas and instructions willingly

- Setting high standards for yourself and others

- Listening without expressing disapproval

- Flexibility

- Asking questions to clarify and identify needs

- Praising the work and efforts of others

- Sharing diverse perceptions on issues

- Commitment to project or task completion

- Talking things out

- Showing tolerance for ambiguity

- Trusting and believing in others

The skills and talents of dynamic followers are equally as important as the skills and talents of dynamic leaders, and coaching within your organization requires you to value the talents and skills of each. Coaching is a process of communication and understanding that has no hierarchical boundaries and that ultimately will demonstrate your leadership and collaboration skills, regardless of your rank.

2. Observe, Listen, Question   When you coach someone, you listen more than you talk: Committed listening is the foundation for masterful coaching. Great coaches believe that people have the intelligence and knowledge that they need if they are to succeed, and that coaching helps them to gain access to it. When you become a coach, you will encourage diverse views and perspectives just to see what is out there, you will stop judging and assuming, you will generate conversations that bring action by asking such questions as, "What is most urgent?" "What is best?" "What are our options?" and "How do we want this to turn out?" Coaching *up* means that you become proactive but not presumptuous, supportive but not ingratiating, communicative but clingy.

3. Watch Yourself Improve   Although it requires self-awareness, emotional maturity, and courage, coaching *up* will improve your job satisfaction, your results, your organization, your team, and your boss.

Coaching one another will allow you to use all of your gifts and talents, honor all of your values and skills, develop relationships based on integrity, maintain high standards, and keep a tight rein on your boundaries. With this comes a sense of fulfillment that you cannot get in any other way, and your fulfillment, or satisfaction, will result in improved performance. That improved performance will improve your team (and teammates), your organization, and your boss.

Coaching Up Strategies

1. Establish an Appropriate Relationship with Your Boss   If you and your boss have had rocky patches in your relationship, review what has not worked, and why. (Refer to Chapter 2 for suggestions.) One of the most important elements in a coaching relationship is that both parties be willing to participate. If there is any baggage or resentment that is creating barriers to your developing a healthy relationship with your boss, you need to determine what it is, prepare a recovery plan, and get ready to take the position of coach (not know-it-all, not expert, not counselor, but coach). Your job as coach is to make your boss look good, and to get the job done more effectively and efficiently.

Since the process of coaching your manager is a format for communication, your manager may not notice that you are coaching her or him. What your manager will notice is that you are always focused on what is right and on how to get it. You might not say, "Hey, boss, let me coach you on that," but you might ask, "What is the best outcome, and what do we need to do to achieve it?"

2. Be Supportive, but Not Competitive   To be supportive is to be loyal, encouraging, and empathetic; to be aware of and sensitive to the goals and barriers that exist; to be willing to ask exploratory questions that may go absolutely nowhere; to be willing to take risks; and to work to help others see options that might not otherwise have been apparent. To be competitive is to take any of those components and make it a platform for aggressively judging the performance of others (typically a win/lose situation). Coaching is neutral, not judgmental or competitive.

Concentrate on providing the kind of support that will help your boss be most effective; this will help you to be more successful as well.

3. Be Certain You Are in Tune with Your Boss's Goals   You may understand that your team has a sales target to reach, a customer satisfaction percentage to achieve, or a zero-error target to accomplish, but have you ever asked your boss what his or her goals are and how you might add value, in addition to your job, in helping him or her reach those goals? Have such a discussion to see how you can become even more valuable to both your organization and your boss.

4. Be Prepared to Speak Up If you do your job well, you have the underlying credibility that you need in order to open discussions when you think things are askew, or when you simply think they could be better. Great coaching requires that you speak the constructive truth, question and explore what is best, and strategize the actions you will take to get to that best.

5. Acknowledge, Affirm, Recognize It is important to acknowledge your boss's and others' efforts and achievements.

- *Let the boss know.* Often your boss hears from his own boss only when there is a problem or a mistake to correct. Sincere praise, encouragement, and appreciation go a long way—even just saying "thank you" leaves a lasting impression. Take time to notice how hard your boss works, and tell her or him that you understand the pressures she or he faces. Praise and acknowledgement should not be saved for extraordinary accomplishments, but should be used every day, with everyone.

- *Make it meaningful.* Acknowledging or praising your boss is not a political maneuver, and it is not designed to make *you* look good. It is a verbal gift; it is empowering, and it must be sincere and meaningful.

6. Be Aware Pay attention to the dynamics of your organization and how your boss operates within those dynamics at the peer level, above, and below. This will give you additional insight into how to add value, be proactive, and ultimately get ahead in your career.

7. Accurately Read Your Boss's Likes and Dislikes   Learning your boss's style in terms of goals and expectations is only half the equation. Learning how your boss handles disagreements, mistakes, priorities, risks, decisions, anger, conflict, and feedback will allow you to coach through issues more easily. The following questions are useful in determining how your boss handles some of those issues in a professional setting. The responses, spoken and unspoken, will give you great clues. Take notes on what you see, hear, and feel about the responses you receive.

- *What is your number one priority this year?* In order to add value, you need to know not only what your boss feels is most urgent, but also what you can do to help your boss reach his or her goals. Look for specifics: If your boss responds with, "Better than I did last year," ask for more detailed information. Look for something like, "I want to produce a 10 percent increase over last year's sales." This type of specificity will help you develop additional questions to identify how you can add value to this area or goal.

- *How will I know if my performance displeases you?* This is about asking for feedback. With my clients, I have found three basic categories concerning feedback:
  1. Those who experience feedback as criticism, seeing it as devastating and humiliating and a validation of their worthlessness
  2. Those who want to hear only praise, nothing that might suggest deficiency (largely due to the response in the previous point)
  3. Those who actually seek out feedback, good or bad, because they see it as a tool that they can use to learn and grow

To be a value-added support to your boss, you need to open the discussion by finding out what is working, and what is not working, in what you are doing. Share how you best receive feedback; ask for straight talk (not sugar-coated) that is focused on shifting behavior (not on personality), using your intellect, your intuition, and your skills. Ask for feedback early and often, but be careful to avoid needing feedback (constantly asking, "How am I doing?" is annoying, not supportive).

- *What should I do if I think you are making a mistake?* This is a critical issue. Ask how your boss would like to be approached—directly or indirectly, in person or by email. Is your boss equally open to receiving feedback (listening carefully, acknowledging your input, and taking corrective action)?

- *During what period of the day do you prefer to have discussions with me?* This sounds silly, but there are times of the day when energy is low and frustrations are high. Whatever your boss states is a "best" time to talk, respect it.

- *How do you handle conflict?* Disagreements, varying perspectives, and differences in style are normal parts of life. Conflict (as in aggressive, win/lose behavior) is unproductive. If you have experienced less-than-effective conflict resolution skills, coach your manager toward skills that are more effective. Share how you best "hear" issues that are in conflict (no snapping, judging, or yelling allowed).

- *What should I do if I sense that you are angry?* Anger can be displayed as fist pounding and door slamming or as silence. Ask your boss how you will know when he or she is angry, and how he or she would prefer that you address him or her at those times. Ask if you can coach him or her through it.

8. Who Moved My Rut?   Webster's defines *rut* as "A track worn by a wheel or by habitual passage of anything; a groove in which anything runs."

Sometimes our jobs, and our lives, fall into a rut and stay there. When you find yourself or your team facing the same old problems and using the same old solutions, when your work no longer demands your very best, or when you no longer look forward to going to work, you're in a rut.

Ruts are familiar and undemanding—and can even be comfortable. However, you pay a high price when you allow yourself to stay in a rut: You actually begin to believe that you are not capable of more and that you don't deserve better, and your results and your job satisfaction plunge.

Pulling yourself out of a rut is not difficult, no matter how deeply you have dug in or how long you've been there. If you, your boss, your team, your organization, or your life is in a rut, use the pause–explore–decide–move process:

- Pause and identify the rut. Give it a name so that you can all identify it when you recognize it.

- Explore the benefits and consequences of this rut. When did the rut start? Why did it come into being? What are the facts and what are the assumptions that keep this rut in place? Why are we in this rut?

- Decide your next move. What are new ways of carrying out this task or this process, new ways of viewing this problem or issue, new ways of acting to shift away from the rut and into effectiveness? Help others, including your boss or your team, to revise their interpretations or assumptions in order to see things in a new way.

- Take action. Once you decide what is most important, act on it. Set a strategy, create a plan, and make the rut disappear.

9. Offer Your Boss Breakthrough Thinking Breakthrough thinking is also called "thinking outside the box." In order for breakthrough thinking to occur, you first must differentiate between thinking and action. Thinking is an intellectual process that is used to solve problems. Action is motion, the steps you take to achieve goals and make things happen. *Breakthrough* thinking is investigating new possibilities and options that result in action, creating something new: new processes or products, new ways to manage information, or new ways for people to work together. Think outside the box, and recommend to your boss new ideas, new processes, new products, and new ways to work together to reach and exceed team goals.

10. Add Value As you coach your boss, you will be learning new skills and unlearning older ones. The goal is to add value to your boss, your team, your organization, and your career. You do this by encouraging diverse views, suspending your assumptions, and generating a conversation for action.

Final Words on Coaching Your Manager

Coaching your manager is a process of communication: listening, sharing, questioning, learning, shifting, and growing—all with an eye toward making your boss look great. And it is a process of self-awareness. In order to be a great coach to others, you must leave all baggage (ego, needs, turf issues) out of the equation, and you must continually choose growth over fear. Coaching focuses on what is best, what is most important, and even what is most urgent, and considers how best to respond to those things, providing you with opportunities to explore ideas and solutions you had not considered before. Ask yourself, your boss, and your team questions like

- What is next?

- Is there a solution here?

- Is this the right time to start this?

- Is there another way?

- What is possible?

- If you knew you would not fail, what would you do now?

Asking questions is sometimes hard, especially in a culture in which you are paid to have the *answers* rather than the questions. Yet it is that very questioning and exploring that will shift you into a healthy relationship with your boss and will create visibility, job satisfaction, and increased productivity.

Concepts to Remember

1. Coach your boss to identify the best possible outcome for every situation.

2. Coach your manager, and your team, through respect, questions, and brainstorming.

3. Be coachable.

4. Lead or follow; both styles make great coaches.

5. Listen more than you talk.

6. Rebuild any rocky relationships and create a strong foundation for coaching your boss.

7. Coaching is neutral, not judgmental or competitive.

8. Be aware of your boss's goals.

9. Speak up.

10. Find a rut and change it.

11. Offer your boss and your team breakthrough thinking.

12. Add value, just for the heck of it.

10

Delivering Results

A coaching client, Peter, shared his results dilemma:

I was hired to help a deteriorating service company right itself after a substantial loss in clients and revenue. I've held the position of VP of operations for less than 1 month, and my six managers are unaware of the layoff that is looming in the very near future. I have to literally force myself to read the weekly reports from my managers; these reports are ostensibly written to advise me of their status and progress, yet they are virtually identical in every way: Each contains the right number of new client contacts, the right number of contacts with existing clients, and an acceptable number of client and customer complaints.

Each of my managers has followed the report process to the letter (by the numbers) yet in the last 3 weeks not one of them has demonstrated to me that he or she is adding any value or delivering any results that really matter. Even though the report template is antiquated, you'd think they'd want me to know what they're doing and how well they're working. I don't know if they are scared or just don't care, but as I prepare for this realignment of resources (and a layoff of three of my managers within the next 2 weeks), I can't help wondering if our clients feel the same ambivalence that I sense in these reports.

Whether you are on site at your employer's office or in a remote location, delivering results *that count* is a key factor in getting ahead. When you are pulled in different directions by multiple priorities and numerous people, and your goals are unclear, you lose focus and control, and your results suffer. Lackluster results may not lead to the termination of your employment, but they will not produce success, satisfaction, or a promotion, either.

All of us work for a reason. The money is certainly part of it, but we also want to make a contribution, enjoy ourselves, learn, develop relationships, participate, be acknowledged and respected, and advance in our careers. Sadly, many organizations focus on an activity-based job description and a once-a-year "you did a good job, see you next year" performance evaluation system, leaving their employees wondering how they will ever move ahead in their careers.

Five Strategies for Delivering Results that Count

There are a number of key strategies that you can use when you are preparing to deliver results that count, including knowing what you do well, knowing what you avoid, knowing what others avoid, time management, awareness of your goals, and aligning your actions with your priorities. When you employ these strategies in connection with your values, you will find that your workday is more fulfilling, your productivity is high, and the quality of your work is better than ever—all components of a get-ahead plan.

I. What You Do Well

In our jobs, we have various goals, tasks, and activities. Some of these we enjoy and do well; some of them we do well, but don't necessarily enjoy; and some of them we don't enjoy and don't do well. If you are going to deliver great results, you will have to identify the category into which each goal, task, or activity falls.

In my corporate sales position, I found that I was good at and enjoyed certain aspects of my job (the consultative sales process, creating solutions, making presentations, developing relationships, and leading); I was competent at *creating* presentations, but I didn't much like it; and I did not enjoy, and was not good at, making cold calls. Since the cold call process was a huge part of that position, I pushed myself and became successful, but I was far from fulfilled.

Through coaching, I came to understand the enjoy/tolerate/dislike factors in my job, and I was able to make shifts and changes that allowed me to focus my career on my values and strengths.

You can identify the parts of the job that you enjoy and are good at for yourself by using Exhibit 10-1 to create a list of what you enjoy and do well. Start with those tasks that you find enjoyable and rewarding, then go on to those that you tolerate, and then to those that you do not like and do not do well.

Exhibit 10-1
Enjoy–Tolerate–Dislike

For each job duty, task, activity, or goal, describe as fully as possible those things that make that job element especially rewarding and enjoyable, those things that you do well but dislike, and those things that make your job especially boring or frustrating. Be as specific as possible.

Activity			Action		
Enjoy	Tolerate	Dislike	Accept	Change	Omit

For each of the items that you tolerate or dislike, evaluate how important that factor is to your job. Can you deliver meaningful results if you do not do these tasks well? Can you deliver meaningful results if you do not like to do these things? Can you participate in training, mentoring, or coaching to change your perception of these duties or to learn to excel at them, or does it make more sense for you to eliminate these duties and tasks from your job? These days, I do only those things that I enjoy and do well; I delegate or eliminate the rest. What can you do with what you do well to reach that same situation?

2. What You Avoid

Avoidance behavior is a tricky thing. It can range from mild procrastination to a full-blown disregard for what needs to be done. When we simply avoid the things that we do not like doing and do not execute well, and we are aware of this, we can make a commitment to learning the skills that are required, shifting behaviors when necessary and taking responsibility for our actions.

Sometimes, though, our avoidance behavior or procrastination is our blind spot—we do not even know that we are avoiding tasks or processes that we need to be completing in order to deliver results. It is critical that you identify and resolve your avoidance or procrastination tendencies.

Putting a Stop to Putting It Off

Take a close look at your behavior—do you dislike and put off similar tasks every week or every month, or do you postpone every task, no matter how small? To get a sense of your level of avoidance, take the Procrastination assessment (Exhibit 10-2) and then consult the scoring key.

Exhibit 10-2
Procrastination

What is your avoidance behavior?

Score yourself on a scale of 1 through 4 for each statement, using the following as a guide:

1 = Not me
2 = Well, maybe I do this
3 = I tend to do this a lot
4 = That's me

_____ I delay finishing certain parts of my job, even though I know they're important.

_____ I postpone starting things I don't particularly like to do—I'll get them done somehow.

_____ When I have a deadline, I wait until the last minute— I work well under pressure.

_____ I manage to find an excuse for not doing the boring parts of my job.

_____ I worry about making a mistake, being right, or being perfect.

_____ When I think a goal is too tough to accomplish, I just don't do it.

_____ Whenever I make a schedule of tasks I don't like, I find other, more important things to do.

_____ Even though I hate myself if I don't get started, I don't get started.

_____ I delay making tough decisions.

_____ I simply avoid those tasks and duties that don't play to my strengths.

_____ Total Score

Scoring Key

10–20: At the lower end of this range, you are paying attention to what needs to be done, and when. At the upper end of the range, you may be avoiding certain tasks, which may result in a time management issue. Keep your schedule tied to your goals, values, and priorities, and keep your boundaries secure.

21–31: You may have some triggers that send you into avoidance or procrastination, and you may have some time management issues as a result. Uncover your underlying issues around avoidance or procrastination, in order that you can develop skills and tools for scheduling, prioritizing, delegating, and learning how to say no, and also do some personal boundary work to keep other people from dumping their stuff on you.

30–40: You are a procrastination machine. If you scored in this range, you'll need to develop the tools and skills to shift out some habits and tendencies. Some ideas for doing so are listed here, but you might want to work with a coach to find out what the underlying causes are for you, and to develop the tools and skills you need.

Underlying Causes of Avoidance and Procrastination   Procrastination and avoidance are problems that face teenagers and adults, males and females, regardless of social group, education, intellect, or background. The consequences of putting things off may range from a minor slowdown to a major catastrophe, and this behavior may become your pathway to a "career cul-de-sac" and may be your single most common time management problem. Since procrastination can be a career-stopper, it is important for you to uncover your pattern of avoidance by reviewing your enjoy/tolerate/dislike worksheet. Identify whether your avoidance behavior is tied to the insignificant (e.g., tasks that are unimportant to the organization and unnecessary for success) or the more crucial (e.g., tasks that are significant, visible, and vital factors in delivering stellar results); then review the following as possible underling sources:

- *Fear.* Some of us avoid or procrastinate because we fear doing the task or carrying out the project at hand. If you find that the work you avoid or put off most requires you to move out of your comfort zone, you may be immobilized by a fear of failure, rejection, being wrong, or embarrassment.

- *Perfectionism.* This is one of the more common reasons for avoiding or procrastinating. Perfectionists avoid starting a task because they worry that they might fall short of their own high standards. A perfectionist will become absorbed in the details, attempting to control every aspect of the task, and ignore the need to move a project along until the very last minute. (They do not have to face their fear of imperfection if the task is not done.)

- *Anxiety over the expectations of others.* Often we avoid or postpone certain tasks because we fear that we will not live up to the expectations of others. This trap is particularly insidious, because by trying to become a bet-

ter person for *other* people, you miss learning who you
really are—that your weaknesses are rich and wonderful teachers, that mistakes are truly golden, and that
those faults of yours are strengths in waiting.

- *Overextended, trying to do too much.* It is possible that
  your avoidance behavior or procrastination tendencies
  stems from overextending yourself. Overdoers have the
  hardest time recognizing themselves as overdoers
  because to them everything is important. "I have 10
  number one priorities!" is a typical mantra of an over-
  doer.

Whether the fundamental cause of your avoidance is fear,
perfectionism, unrealistic expectations, or overextending, it is in
your best interest professionally and personally to get this issue
resolved—forever. Identify your barrier by catching yourself in
the act of procrastinating or avoiding, and apply the three-step
process described in Chapter 5:

PAUSE: What is going on here?

EXPLORE: Why am I feeling this way?

DECIDE: What is the best thing to do right now?

Regardless of its source, avoidance behavior can be an artifi-
cial defense against the challenging or difficult parts of your
career and your life. You need to be willing to face those areas
that are not functioning well and deal with them head-on; in the
end, this will provide the professional success and personal fulfillment that comes from an aware, balanced life.

3. What Your Peers Avoid

This is easy: Observe (without judgment) what your peers seem
to avoid. Do your peers avoid these tasks or projects because they
are inconsequential, or because they do not enjoy them? Are these
tasks or projects essential to delivering great results? Watch what
it is that your peers *don't* do, and if it is important, do it (and do
it well).

4. Time Management

If you have ever wondered why you find that some days zip by and
without your touching one item on your to-do list, it is time to
evaluate how you choose to spend your time. ("I don't choose, it
just happens!"—baloney!) While we all have days when constantly
changing priorities and interruptions make time management difficult, we *do* choose what gets our attention. You can choose to
create an efficient and flexible schedule based on your priorities;
doing so requires that you work with the following strategies.

Time Do you really know what you do all day? We each have
24 hours in each day and 7 days in each week, so where does the
time go?

   You may have seen or completed a time study before, but this
is still one of the best methods of determining where the time
goes (see Exhibit 10-3). For several days, keep track of what you
do with your time, including everything from commuting time
to sleeping, and everything in between. You can add special categories to your time study to identify more easily the amount of
time spent answering emails, attending meetings, running
errands, and so on. Include everything that applies to you, and

Exhibit 10-3
What Have You Done All Day?

Item	Monday			Tuesday			Wednesday			Thursday			Friday			Saturday			Sunday		
	Start	End	Total	Start	End	Total	Start	End	Total	Start	End	Total	Start	End	Total	Start	End	Total	Start	End	Total

Family Time

Item
With children
With spouse/partner
Breakfast
Lunch
Dinner
Grooming
Commute
Chores/errands
Gym
TV

At Work

Item
Phone calls—outgoing
Phone calls—incoming
Answering email
Meetings
Drop-in discussions
Lunch hour/break
Managing staff
Writing/compiling reports

keep track of the time you spend on each item. Once you have completed your study for 1 week, stack-rank your list by the number of hours you spent on each item (highest to lowest). That is your current priority list.

Does your actual priority list match the priority list on your desk? Do the actions you take on a daily basis match your real priorities? If not, take the time to identify what you are doing that is wasteful of your time and energy, and make some changes.

Delegate If you are spending time on things that could be handled by someone else, it is time for you to delegate. The objective of delegation is

- To get the job done by someone else, giving that person a clear description of what needs to be done, by when, and to what standard.

- To give the person the authority to complete the task or project (including making decisions and responding to situations that may arise without referring back to you).

- To maintain a level of responsibility. You are primarily responsible for ensuring that the task is completed on time and correctly. If the task or project is late or unsuccessful, you cannot point the finger: You delegated, but you may have picked the wrong person for the job.

How to Delegate

1. Identify the tasks or projects that can be delegated. *Hint:* Never delegate the following if they are your primary job duties:

- Hiring
- Firing
- Pay issues
- Policy development or enforcement

2. Identify the correct person to perform the task or project.

3. Coach the person to do well. Explain the task or project clearly and check to be sure that he or she understands the desired results and timeframe, but leave wiggle room in the task description so that your delegate can use his or her own ingenuity and initiative.

4. Make sure that the delegate has the authority to do the job properly.

5. Keep in touch with the person to provide support, and request periodic updates on progress (but do not micromanage).

6. Acknowledge your delegate for a job well done.

> *I not only use all the brains I have, but all I can borrow.*
> —*Woodrow Wilson*

Avoid Distractions   In the traditional office, there are hundreds of distractions; in a home office, there are even more.

Drop-in distractions can waste an enormous amount of time. If you have a constant stream of well-intentioned colleagues and subordinates interrupting your concentration and focus, stop them. You can close your office door or, for those working in cubicles, hang out a "stoplight" of colored paper (red: no interruptions, please; yellow: I'm busy, but if it's important, come in; green: I am available to speak with you). Share this system with your cube-mates so that everyone understands its meaning and will respect it.

Email messages and phone calls can provide a constant stream of interruptions, yet it is important that you address each one in order to maintain your visibility and your positive reputation. You do not have to answer them when they arrive, though. Keep emails and phone calls from overtaking your day by creating a process for determining which are most urgent and which can be delegated or deleted. Set aside a block of time each day (say, 30 minutes each morning, 30 minutes at midday, and 30 minutes before you leave) to read and respond to email messages and return phone calls.

5. Goals and Priorities That Deliver Results

Traditional job descriptions have been conscientiously written to address legal issues and to define what is expected of an employee in terms of activities. What we often do not learn from our job descriptions is what results are required, what skills (technical and behavioral) are necessary if we are to deliver those results, and what actions should be taken to produce the desired outcome.

A traditional performance review is an equally dismal tool for employees—an employee learns, often for the first time, how he or she measures up, based on a mistaken assumption that both employee and manager perceive the job, and the desired results, in the same way. Where does the employee learn the specifics of the results that are required if he or she is to be successful, the skills that are needed in order to be technically proficient and behaviorally competent, and the actions that support the priorities?

Developing a Results Orientation

Here is a fact: If you want to improve your results, you have to better define the work that needs to be done. As when you wrote your vision and mission statements, you first have to know where you want to be (desired results) and assess what it will take to get there (required skills); only then can you establish your action steps to ensure that you deliver results that count.

Complete the Results Profile (Exhibit 10-4) by identifying the following criteria for your own job:

1. *Desired results.* These are the measurable, significant business results that are deliverable through your job. Working with your past performance appraisals, corporate and team goals, and your boss's goals, identify as many potential results for your job as you can. Ask yourself, "What does outstanding look like in this job?" and "What does fully competent look like in this job?" Understand the difference between the two answers, and strive for outstanding.

2. *Technical skills required.* Identify the technical skills (hardware, software, job-specific, or industry knowledge) that are necessary if you are to be successful in delivering these results. You may add to this list after you have completed the Actions to Take section (item 5).

Exhibit 10-4
Results Profile

SUMMARY OF IDEAL RESULTS AND THE SKILLS, SUPPORT, AND ACTIONS NEEDED TO MAKE THEM HAPPEN

POSITION _____ DATE _____

Desired Results	Technical Skills Required	Behavioral Skills Required	Support or Assistance Needed From	Actions to Take	Target Date	Date Completed

3. *Behavioral skills required.* Identify the behaviors, tendencies, or skills that are required in order to deliver
   results; these might perhaps include strategic thinking,
   attention to detail, persuasion, negotiation, speaking,
   conflict resolution, or customer relationship skills. List
   all the behavioral skills that apply to delivering the
   results required for success in your position. You may
   want to review these behavioral skills again after you
   have completed the Actions to Take section (item 5).

4. *Support or assistance.* Identify the people, skills, or things
   that you need to learn or have available in order to
   achieve the results you desire. This might include additional training on technical matters, a new software
   program, or support on behavioral shifts from a coach.

5. *Actions to take.* Once you know what has to be done
   (the results) and the abilities required to do it (the skill
   sets), the actions to take are relatively easy to identify.
   All of your key results must be driven by specific activities or actions that will guide you to achieve your goals.
   Each result may have five to eight activities or actions;
   list them specifically.

6. *Target date.* No plan for success is complete without a
   deadline. Identify what needs to be done, and by when.
   Then make a calendar of your action steps.

7. *Completion date.* Keep track of your completed tasks,
   take the opportunity to celebrate milestones, and prepare for the next steps.

Once you have identified these key areas of your job, take the opportunity to review the list with your boss, and make any adjustments required. Completing this plan will give you a strong foundation from which you can track your progress and success. You will avoid mistaking activity for results, you will be able to clearly connect specific actions with specific results (so that you can repeat them), and you will know what needs to be done, how it needs to be done, and when it needs to be done.

Final Thoughts on Delivering Results

Peter's dilemma, described at the beginning of this chapter, shows what it is like to be on the receiving end when employees are focused simply on getting by, rather than on delivering results. The managers' ambivalence toward their work made his job more difficult and made their continued employment questionable.

In a corporate environment that is shifting from "do something, even if it's wrong" to "do what is best," delivering results *that count* is critical. You can carry out the activities covered by your job description and you can follow the recommendations in your performance evaluation to the letter, but until you identify *what* must be done and *how* it must be done (technically and behaviorally), *when* you do it doesn't really matter.

Know how your boss and your company define "results," then go a step further: How can you deliver the best results ever? How can you add value to your boss, your company, and yourself, while still maintaining balance in your life? Focus first on the *what*, then on the *how*, and only then on the *when*.

Concepts to Remember

1. Choose growth over fear.

2. Focus on what you do well and leverage the rest.

3. Put a stop to putting it off.

4. Be aware of your avoidance behavior.

5. Learn from the avoidance behavior of others.

6. Choose how you will spend your time.

7. Delegate wisely.

8. Manage distractions.

9. To deliver stellar results, you must clearly define the work that needs to be done.

10. Focus first on the *what*, then on the *how*, and only then on the *when*.

11

When, Why, and How to
Ask for a Raise

*In 1988, when I had been working for the same Fortune 500
company for about 8 years, I learned that my male counterpart
was earning $10,000 more than I was. The fact that this col-
league and I were friends made the situation more difficult for
me. I was familiar with his background, education, and experience, and we were alike in many ways. There was certainly
a gender difference, but my results were better, and I was ready
to make more money.*

*So, I did a little research by calling contacts with competi-
tors for salary information. Then I waited for the right time,
made an appointment with my boss, wore my best "power suit,"
marched into my boss's office, and said: "I have been in my
director role for 2 years, with outstanding results. [I showed him
a breakdown of my results for the last year, a number of letters*

of appreciation from our company's largest clients, and a goal list for the coming year.]

"I have a question and a request. First, the question: Can you help me understand why Bob earns $10,000 more than I do? My tenure is longer by 6 years, and we are similar in background and experience. My results are rated as outstanding, my performance evaluations are consistently outstanding, and my salary is less. If there are critical issues keeping me at this below-grade level, I'd like to know what they are so that I can work to improve. If the salary difference is a quirk of process, I'd like to reach parity, so let me know.

"Now the request: I think my results and the cost savings to the company warrant a salary increase of 10 percent. My research shows that within our company and within our industry, the salary range is $75,000 to $95,000, and a 10 percent increase in salary, once parity has been reached, will put me there."

My boss, a man of few words, said, "Impressive. Let me do some checking and I'll get back to you." Later that day, back to me he came, with a retroactive pay increase covering the $10,000 shortage plus a 12 percent salary increase.

Asking for a salary increase is difficult, whether there is an inconsistency in the application of the salary plan or you simply believe that you have earned a raise. This process worked for me in 1988, and a similar, but upgraded, process continues to work for my clients now.

When you have been with your company long enough to have demonstrated that you have made an impact, prepare to ask for a raise. Before you ask, though, you will have to know why and how to ask, and for how much. Here are the basics to remember.

1. Do Your Homework

What is your company's policy on salary increases?

Find out how salary adjustments are handled in your organization. If no employee handbook exists (or if the handbook does not address salary increases), contact your human resources representative and ask for a copy of the policy. You will want to consider the following:

- How does the company's compensation program function? Are salary increases given only at performance evaluation time or never at performance evaluation time? Do not be discouraged if your salary request plans fall outside of the policy parameters (or if no policy exists). Knowing the company's standard process will help you with your strategy.

- What is the maximum raise given? If, as in my case in 1988, you need to bring your salary up to level and you also feel that you have earned a merit increase, you need to know what hurdles you will have to surmount before you go to your boss. If your company has a policy against salary increases in excess of 5 percent, you need to know this before you ask. If you deserve a salary increase in excess of the maximum, be prepared to prove it.

- How is your performance evaluated? What yardstick is used to measure your performance? Does it correspond with your own evaluation criteria for your performance? If there is a difference between what you think is outstanding performance and your boss's definition, a raise will be difficult to negotiate. Get the facts.

- What do other (lateral) positions earn? In some organizations, this information may be considered confidential, but it will not hurt to ask. Most forward-thinking companies recognize that this information is vital to anyone who is interested in career development planning.

2. You Deserve a Raise Because ...

Why do you deserve a raise?

What are the special skills that you have, the new responsibilities you have been given, and the exceptional results that you have produced that warrant an increase in salary? If you have a sense of your boss's goals, how your boss defines success, and the results required for success in your position, you are prepared to make your case.

You will want to ensure that you are being evaluated against your current job description and on the basis of results delivered, and you will want to demonstrate a valid *business* reason why you should be paid more. Create a list of your accomplishments, including any of your ideas that resulted in cost cuts, increased sales, time savings, and creativity. Give specific examples with numbers (facts) that show your achievements.

As you create your list, organize your accomplishments logically so that you are familiar with them and are comfortable recalling them during your meeting. This will help you to develop a follow-up memo to your boss confirming your discussion (see item 9). Prepare a clean copy of this list to hand to your boss during your discussion.

3. How Much

Get the facts. You will want an estimate of the salary range for your position within your current organization and also the value of your position on the open market. This is important: If you simply ask for a raise, your boss may give you a nominal increase that will eliminate your opportunity to negotiate. Have a specific figure in mind—percentage and dollar—so that you can negotiate. Use the resources given in Chapter 15 to research salaries— and remember, the more information you have, the more likely it is that your boss will accept your request.

4. Barriers

What are some potential objections?

When you ask for a raise on the same day that your boss is discussing a layoff or your company posted its worst quarterly results ever, you may get the answer, "We can't afford it." While part of this problem is timing (see item 5), it is important for you to become aware of the potential hurdles you may have to overcome. List each potential hurdle, and create a statement to leverage it.

5. Timing Is Everything

You will want to ask for a raise at a time when your company has posted record profits, or your department has just met a goal as a result of your efforts, or you just beat an important deadline and your boss is relaxed and on a personal high. Avoid those times when mass layoffs are underway, you have been advised of an error in your judgment, or your boss is having a bad day. Consider the following timing recommendations:

- If the standard practice is merit increases during annual review time, how far in the future is that date? If it is several months away, you might want to consider asking just after a stunning success.

- If your job responsibilities have increased, but your salary has not, the timing might be just right. (You would think that the money would follow the increase in responsibility, but this often does not happen.)

- Know your boss's high-energy time—is it morning or afternoon? Pay attention, and time your request accordingly.

- Know your company's financial situation. Use the resources in Chapter 15 to research the company's financial history and status before you ask for that increase.

6. The Do's

Asking for a raise is frightening for us if we define ourselves by our salaries. In fact, your salary is a reflection of how your company values the services you provide to it, not a reflection of you. Getting a raise is an objective business decision, so approach it as such.

Summarize what you did, how you did it, and the benefits

that resulted for your employer. Add comments on your goals and plans for next year.

If you are worried about being off base in your request, you might start with a question such as

> *"I'm interested in asking for a raise. How would you do that if you were me?"*

> *"I'd like to talk to you about my performance and salary. Can I have an hour of your time this week?"*

Once you have opened the conversation, you could continue with

> *"I saved the company $50,000 by streamlining the service delivery process. Since I created and implemented a process that allows our clients to get information on their orders before speaking to their client representative, our service rating has increased to 100 percent for 8 months running. I've also exceeded targets on sales and managed to a tight budget consistently.*
> *"I think my results put me in line for an increase of 6 percent—this fits within the company's guidelines, and it would bring me to the salary level that others in similar positions are making these days."*

Be prepared for your boss to say that he or she will "think about it," which may be code for "I'll have to check my budget and with HR." Do not beg, grovel, or threaten—and never say, "I need the money." The focus must be on the raise you *deserve*, not the raise you *need*. Close with a "thank you," whether you get the raise on the spot or not.

7. The Don'ts

- *Do not say that you need the money.* You are demonstrating a compelling business reason for a salary increase, and it has nothing to do with your wanting a new car or a trip to Europe. Your company does not care about your material needs, but it does care about your value to it and to its owners and shareholders. Show that you have earned the raise.

- *Do not be adversarial, difficult, immature, or unprofessional.* If you are defensive, angry, unreasonable, sobbing, or whiny, your boss will probably end the conversation immediately. This is a business discussion, with both sides trying to reach agreement. Keep it professional.

- *Do not issue an ultimatum.* If you threaten to leave if the salary increase is denied, be prepared to back it up. Saying, "If I don't get this [raise, promotion, bonus], I will quit" will probably invoke a response of, "OK, have your written resignation on my desk by the end of the day."

   Even if the company says, "Oh, my! Please don't go!" you have showed your hand. Your boss knows that you lack loyalty and are probably hunting for your next job anyway.

   If you deserve a raise, a bonus, or a promotion, and you are denied it, you can always decide to leave, but that decision should be separate from the discussion about your salary.

- *Do not demand to be paid the same as your coworkers.* When I approached my boss concerning the disparity in pay, I asked a question for clarification: "Why?" My justification for my merit increase was my performance, and I addressed the parity issue separately. My goal was to both reach parity *and* get an increase, yet I made no demands.

  If you are aware of a salary difference between you and your peers, find out why the difference exists. Commit to learning any skills or behaviors mentioned as reasons for the difference, and be ready to revisit your salary increase once you have learned them.

  Not every parity issue is discrimination, so ask smart questions and keep your initial conversations focused on the raise you have earned.

8. Schedule the Meeting

Ask for a meeting at a time that will be convenient for your boss, and do not keep the meeting topic a secret. Say, "I'd like to get on your calendar for about 30 minutes to discuss my performance and salary. Are you free Tuesday morning?"

9. Follow Up

After your meeting with your boss, follow up with a memo confirming your discussion (this will help if your boss must justify the salary increase through other channels). Start with a thank you for your boss's time and consideration, and reiterate your accomplishments, referring to the list you prepared. (Attach another copy; this one goes in your personnel file.) If you and your boss have agreed on an effective date for your increase, mention it in your memo. If not, request one (and schedule a follow-up to make sure it is done).

What to Do When You Ask for, but Don't Get a Raise

If you ask for a raise, but it is denied, you have an opportunity to find out what is missing and get it.

- If your boss disagrees about the financial value of your position to the organization ("We don't pay counselors that much"), you may have asked for an increase that is outside of a predetermined salary band. Go back and research salary survey information, and regroup.

- If your boss disagrees about your performance, ask for feedback on what it is you need to learn in order to get the raise you want. Prepare a schedule of goals (using the Results Profile, Exhibit 10-4, and the Goal Worksheet, Exhibit 6-4) to outline the actions you will take and when you will take them.

- If your boss responds with a no without an explanation, again ask for feedback. If your boss still holds back, let her or him know (gently) that you would like to take the discussion to the next level, or to Human Resources. This is risky: Your boss may feel that her or his authority is being challenged. Be thoughtful in your request, and make it clear that you are seeking feedback and information on getting a raise that you feel you have earned. Never do this without informing your boss (you do not need permission); your boss will find out whether you tell her or him or not, and it is better that your boss hear it from you.

- A negative response to a well-planned and well-deserved request for increase may be your wake-up call. If there is not sufficient room for growth at your current company, it may be time to move on. See "When All Else Fails" in Chapter 13.

Final Thoughts on Getting a Raise

If you have earned a salary increase, ask for it. Knowledge of your strengths, skills, and values; an honest assessment of your performance; and a keen understanding of the financial value of your job on the open market and the financial value of your position to the company will prepare you to make the right moves. Do the research, demonstrate your confidence, muster your courage, and take action: Ask for the raise you deserve.

Concepts to Remember

1. If you deserve a raise, ask for it.

2. Do your homework before asking for a raise.

3. Find out your company policy on salary increases.

4. Be prepared to state why you've earned the raise.

5. Do research on how much of a raise to request—both internally and externally.

6. Identify your potential hurdles.

7. Choose the right time to ask.

8. Don't say you need the money.

9. Don't be adversarial.

10. Don't threaten to quit.

11. Don't demand a raise.

12

How to Get a Promotion

In June 1974, Marty had been the director of personnel for 3 years when his boss, Pam, decided to move on from her VP spot to another organization. At the time Pam gave her formal notice, everyone was quite surprised. She was well respected, knowledgeable, and loyal: a lifer.

Despite the surprise over her resignation, though, the shifts required to fill the opening in the organization took place in less than 1 hour. Marty accepted a promotion to VP of personnel; Jackie, who had formerly been assistant director, advanced to Marty's old role of director. And I gladly accepted a promotion from personnel clerk to assistant director of personnel after only 3 weeks on the job—mostly because I was there.

"There" was also a good place to be 1 month later, when Jackie resigned from her director position to head back to college. Only 6 weeks into this job, I had had two promotions.

In the past, the most important criterion for achieving a promotion was showing up every day—seniority was the most direct road to promotability.

As the 1970s turned into the 1980s, pay for performance was the name of the game, and the tenure-based promotion system was slowly replaced by a merit-based promotion system—which was also flawed. In the merit-only system, little regard was paid to the skills and knowledge needed for the new position—only how well the candidate did in his or her current spot was considered. This system allowed the promotion of many underprepared and underqualified people into management positions as a reward for doing well, as my client Lin attests:

I accepted the position of regional corporate sales manager with a major lender about 6 weeks ago. During the interview process, I thought my manager, Linda, was more task-oriented than strategic, but I needed a job, and I wanted to believe that she knew what she was doing.

After a few days on the job, Linda shared with me that she had been executive secretary to the president of a small lender prior to its purchase by the larger lender—and that as a reward for sticking with the organization during a complicated merger process, she had been promoted from executive secretary to vice president of corporate lending. She told me that she had earned her promotion because she had been with the smaller lender for 15 years, this had been her first and only job, and she had maintained an excellent performance record the entire time.

Now I have a boss who has never made a corporate sale, never met with a client, never managed to do a budget, never planned a regional marketing strategy, and never managed professional staff. Because she doesn't really know the process, she micromanages every task. I think I've made a big mistake accepting this job.

Luck

A recent survey by J. Howard & Associates found that 39 percent of the employees responding believe that the current road to promotability is still merit only: Do well, and you will move ahead. Over half of the employees responding believe that promotability is based on other factors in addition to merit, including personal connections, seniority (only younger workers felt this way), and luck (when preparation and opportunity meet).

Getting a promotion takes much more than just being there, doing well in your current job, having great personal connections, or even being lucky. It takes all of that, and more. It takes

- A complete understanding of your strengths, skills, and values (self-awareness)

- An appreciation of how you are perceived by others (awareness)

- A high level of positive and accurate visibility

- A demonstration of your knowledge of corporate priorities

- A reputation for being trustworthy

- A proven ability to lead others, and to follow well, too

- A willingness to take smart risks and openly learn from your mistakes

- An ability to make it easy for the company to promote you by being great at what you do: by thinking, not just doing

The Road to Promotability

There are two critical components of promotability:

1. You have to be the best you can be.

2. Your best must be exactly what is needed, and wanted, in your current organization. If it is not, then it may be time to move on (see Chapter 13).

Let's check on the first component: Are you the best you can be right now? To gain a sense of your starting point, determine your Promotability Quotient (Exhibit 12-1), and then analyze your score.

> *Exhibit 12-1*
> *Promotability Quotient*
> What is your Promotability Quotient? The following questions relate to your visibility, reputation, values, skills, and strengths—and the more honest you are with your answers, the more quickly you will recognize your next steps.

	Yes	No	
1.			Do you have a written career strategy for the next
a.	___	___	1 year
b.	___	___	5 years
c.	___	___	None
2.			Have you completed a written version of your
a.	___	___	Values
b.	___	___	Needs
c.	___	___	Strengths and skills
3.	___	___	Do you know what your next logical step is with your current company?
4.	___	___	Have you identified the skill set required for the next level?
5.	___	___	Do you have those required skills?
6.	___	___	Do you have a record of success in your current job, including taking smart risks?
7.	___	___	Have you been assigned to participate in or head up important projects and task forces that are visible within the company?
8.	___	___	Are you known to be respectful, knowledgeable, influential, and productive within your organization?
9.	___	___	Do you work well with your boss?
10.	___	___	Are you known to your boss and his peers as the "go to" person when extra brainpower is needed?

11. ___ ___ Is your company financially healthy?

12. ___ ___ Are you aware of the history of promotions in your company?

13. ___ ___ Do you fit the profile?

14. ___ ___ Do you have a solid network of peers, subordinates, and managers within your organization?

15. ___ ___ Are you a knowledge broker, with resources and experts available to you?

16.   Would you be called

   a. ___ ___ A gossip

   b. ___ ___ An egomaniac

   c. ___ ___ A control freak

   d. ___ ___ Out of it

   e. ___ ___ Inflexible

   f. ___ ___ Unreliable

   g. ___ ___ Irresponsible

   h. ___ ___ Uncooperative

   i. ___ ___ None of these, nor any other negative tag

17.   Do you read trade papers or magazines to keep up with your industry?

   a. ___ ___ Once per week

   b. ___ ___ Once per month

   c. ___ ___ Once in a while

   d. ___ ___ Never

18. When was the last time you attended a class to brush up your skills (or learn new ones) outside of the office?

a. ___ ___ Within the last 6 months

b. ___ ___ Within the last 12 months

c. ___ ___ Never

19. When was the last time you asked your boss about the skills or talents necessary for success and promotion?

a. ___ ___ Within the last 6 months

b. ___ ___ Within the last 12 months

c. ___ ___ Never

Score:

		Yes	No				Yes	No
1.	a.	10			13.		10	−10
	b.		−5		14.		10	−10
	c.		−15		15.		10	−10
2.	a.	10	−10		16.	a.		−10
	b.	10	−10			b.		−10
	c.	10	−10			c.		−10
3.		10	0			d.		−10
4.		10	0			e.		−10
5.		10	0			f.		−10
6.		10	0			g.		−10
7.		10	0			h.		−10
8.		10	−10			i.	10	
9.		10	−10		17.	a.	10	
10.		10	−5			b.	5	
11.		10	−10			c.	1	
12.		10	−10			d.	−15	

		Yes	No			Yes	No
18.	a.	10		19.	a.	10	
	b.	5			b.	5	
	c.	−15			c.	−15	

_____ Total Score

Scoring Key

0–50 You may be working at a job, but you have not yet defined a career. Roll up your sleeves and go back to the basics. You will need a genuine desire to succeed, a lot of hard work, and the strategies that follow.

51–100 You may know the general direction of your career, but your foundation is unsteady. Again, go back to basics (strengths, skills, needs, and values) and redefine the gap between where you are right now and where you want to be.

101–150 You have identified a more specific direction for yourself and your career, and you are ready to focus and move ahead. Identify the categories in the assessment where you scored the lowest and honestly identify what it will take to learn those skills or shift your reputation in those areas.

151–200 You are right on track in developing a reputation and a career that will set you apart in a competitive marketplace. Upgrading some areas will drive you forward more quickly. Check your lowest scores and work to improve in those areas as you prepare to ask for your promotion.

201–220 Congratulations! You have a strong sense of self-awareness, you know your strengths and limitations, you have a solid reputation, you understand the expectations of your company and your boss, and you can quickly implement your strategy for being promoted.

Prepare for Action

Gather the following worksheets from earlier in this book:

- Values Worksheet (Exhibit 1-3), completed

- Enjoy–Tolerate–Dislike (Exhibit 10-1), completed

- Results Profile (Exhibit 10-4), a fresh blank form

- Goal Worksheet (Exhibit 6-4), several blank forms

Five Strategies to a Promotion
I. Evaluate and Interpret

If you are to get a promotion, it is important for you to have an accurate view of how others see you, over and above your work product (which must be brilliant). If you scored below 175 on the Promotability Quotient, review your Needs Analysis Form (Exhibit 1-2) to identify and remove behavioral barriers. If you are having trouble identifying your barriers using this form, consider working with a coach. Many good coaches offer pro bono coaching, some will barter, and others work for a monthly fee. Use the coach referral resource in Chapter 15 to find a coach who will fit within your budget. Getting a handle on any barriers will help you quickly move ahead in your career.

If necessary, review the rebound plan outlined in Chapter 1 to rebuild your reputation in preparation for a promotion. If a rebound is not possible with your current employer, see Chapter 13, "If, When, and How to Leave Your Job."

2. Review Your Enjoy–Tolerate– Dislike Worksheet

One of the biggest mistakes people make when working on their career advancement plan is to act only in order to avoid aggravation rather than moving toward a goal. When I asked a client about his career plans recently, he said, "I will not be working *here* this time next year." While that may very well be true, this was really a statement of frustration that demonstrated his desire to move *away* from something (a job he didn't like) rather than his being drawn *toward* something (his strengths, skills, and values). Moving away from something will not keep you from repeating the pattern; making smart choices about what works for you based on your values, strengths, and skills will.

Part of the process of planning well is to convert your statements of frustration into positive requirements *for you*. Take your Enjoy-Tolerate-Dislike list from Exhibit 10-1, and reformulate each statement of frustration into a positive statement, starting with "I work best with." For example, if your Dislike list stated, "My boss was a micromanager," you might list a new requirement for your next job as, "I work best with a manager who delegates well and demonstrates trust in his employees."

In Exhibit 12-2, Shifting Problems to Potential, list *each issue* identified in the Tolerate and Dislike columns of Exhibit 10-1, and convert those issues into affirmative statements, or standards, drawing you toward your values, strengths, and skills. Complete your P2P inventory by listing the items you enjoy, preparing an "I work best" sentence for each.

Exhibit 12-2
Shifting Problems to Potential

List your job dissatisfiers or statements of frustration, and reframe them into positive requirements for a job you will love.

ISSUE	STATEMENT
Boss was a micromanager	I am best managed by a boss who delegates well and demonstrates trust in his employees.

3. Your Objective

Before you can convince anyone else about your career direction
and purpose, you must define it for yourself. Determining your
objective is a prerequisite to landing your next position. To clearly
identify your objective, answer the following questions:

- What is my specialty, product, or service?

- What need or problem within my organization does my
  specialty address?

- What is the next most logical step in my career?

- How does this progression match my skills, strengths,
  and values?

Now, using the answers to these questions, what are the three
most likely titles for your next position?

- _____

- _____

- _____

Compare your list of likely target positions against your previously identified values, skills, and strengths, and ask,

- Which of these positions is available (or will soon be
  available) within my current organization?

- Which position fits best with my long-range career goals?

- Which position is best for my life-balance goals?

- Which position fulfills my standards from my P2P inventory?

- Of the three target positions, which best uses my skills, strengths, and values, and which will allow me to leverage any weaknesses?

- What are the biggest obstacles to my getting the promotion?

Use the answers to these questions to help you narrow down your list to one target position. Now you are ready to define the new position in relation to your skill base, and to strategize how to get it.

4. Your New Results Profile

When you completed your Results Profile on your current job (Exhibit 10-4), you were able to identify the results, skills, actions, and support that you needed in order to be truly successful and deliver meaningful results. Now you will complete a Results Profile for your next job. This will require some research, some observation, and some guesswork.

Find a copy of the job description for the position you have identified as your next step. (Ask your human resources department or your boss.) True, the job description will probably give you only the activities to be undertaken and not the results required, but it is a launch pad for identifying the gap between where you are right now and where you want to be next.

Once you have reviewed the job description, talk with people who are already in the position you have targeted, even if this means talking to your boss. You might say, "I've been thinking about my career plan, and I'd like to investigate the skills required for the X position. I thought you'd be a good person to help me."

Then formulate a list of questions that will help you identify what it will take for you to get that job. You will certainly want to know about the desired results, but you may also want to know

- What is the most challenging and fun part of that job?

- What is the most frustrating part?

- How do you see this position growing in the next 5 years?

- What advice would you give to someone in my position?

- What are some of the interim steps necessary for a person to reach that position?

A Note on Asking Your Boss:
   Good leaders will welcome your inquiry as a sign of your for-ward-thinking career planning. Some bosses will be less accommo-

dating, however, perhaps because they are fearful of your possibly outperforming them. You will have to make the call here, but if your boss is not willing to discuss your promotability plans with you, you will have to work around him or her—a difficult task. If this is your experience, also read "When All Else Fails" in Chapter 13.

Once you have your answers, complete a new Results Profile for your target position based on the job description and the discussions you have had with people who are already in the job, your boss, his boss, Human Resources, and people at peer level with the target position. Focus on the first four columns of the worksheet: Desired Results, Technical Skills Required, Behavioral Skills Required, and Support or Assistance Needed.

For each desired result, you either will or will not have the qualifications, experience, education, and skills. If you do not, you should include in the Actions to Take column the actions you will take in order to gain the experience, skill, or education needed. Be certain to list your target dates, and to enter the date when you complete each action (see item 5).

The following are some actions you might consider for your target position:

- Increase or enhance your internal network in order to gain information and visibility (for instance, to learn if there's a job possibility coming up).

- Learn new skills. If your promotability is slowed by the absence of a skill that you have not yet mastered, take action. Find a way to audit a class, get a certificate or degree, or even volunteer for a nonprofit in the area you are seeking.

- Demonstrate initiative. Sometimes an obvious candidate for a promotion is seen as doing "only what is expected" in her or his current role, and so is quickly out of the running. Make sure you are seen in your current position as qualified, competent, and resourceful.

If you already have the required qualifications, your entry in the Actions to Take column will be proof sources: What proof can you offer that you do in fact have the required background? Look for ways to present your skills and qualifications in numbers—dollars saved, percent of increased sales, number of units processed, size of budget managed. (You will use this later.)

5. Ready, Set, Goals

For each desired result requiring you to take a specific action, prepare a Goal Worksheet. Be clear, concise, and real about your goals. Also, be certain to allow for additional support, internal or external, to assist you in reaching your goals. Next, determine your deadline, remembering that it is easier to learn new skills and develop visibility before the need arises. Then prepare a calendar of the tasks and supporting activities, and you are ready to go.

You will know best if you have what it will take to get a promotion. If you are missing key components, but your company culture supports on-the-job learning, go for it. If your company does not support promoting those who are ready, willing, and able to learn, you can work on acquiring the required skills and education while

1. Keeping an eye on the next round of promotions

2. Looking for a sensible lateral move to improve your breadth of knowledge

3. Looking outside of your organization for a job you would love

4. Doing all of the above

Ask for the Promotion

When you are ready with everything you need for a promotion, it is time to ask for the promotion. Do not wait for the opening to happen, and do not hint at it; ask early, and be clear about your direction. As backup, have the following materials available when you make your request:

- A summary of your current accomplishments

- A summary of the requirements (results, technical skills, and behavioral skills) for the new position

- A summary of your skill set and how you meet those requirements

- An awareness of the salary package you want to negotiate

Watch your timing. The day your boss received a poor performance review or the company announced poor results is just not a good day to ask for a promotion. Ask for your promotion on a day when things are going well, and at a time of day when your boss is energetic (do not ask at 3 P.M. on a Friday, ask mid-morning on a Tuesday or Wednesday).

Prepare a script (not memorized, just a cheat-sheet) to open the discussion with your boss:

"I'd like to have that job in San Francisco. I have a list of the skills I think are needed, and I believe I am ready. I'd like to make sure you think I've covered the bases, and talk about next steps."

Approach your manager early so that you can collaborate with him or her, and pay close attention to his or her responses. Remember, your promotion will create a gap in your boss's organization chart, so part of your discussion will cover recommendations for your own replacement.

When You Asked, but Were Not Promoted

In corporate America, getting a promotion is similar to the childhood game of Musical Chairs: Someone is not going to be able to grab a seat when the music stops. If you are the one left standing, this is a good time to rewind, review, and get back on your road to success. Review the following questions, and analyze any gaps:

1. If the position was posted, did you comply with the application process required by your company?

2. If the position was not posted, did the right people know about your interest? Who did, who did not, and who should have?

3. Did you have a realistic perception of the requirements of the job? During any part of the promotional interview process, were there questions asked that left you feeling uncomfortable? What were they?

4. Did you and the hiring manager have a difference of opinion about your readiness for the job? If so, was the manager's perception accurate? If it was inaccurate, what was the reason for that perception?

5. Did your current boss have a need to keep you where you are?

6. Did your reputation support your promotion plan?

Take the time to review your answers to these questions, and to deal with any anger or frustration with the situation, your company, or yourself that you may have. You will not move forward in your career if the weight of resentment is dragging you down; but do not cover it up, do not try to hide it, and do not blame it on someone else. Use your self-awareness and self-management skills (Chapter 1) to accept what has happened, even if you do not like it.

Once you have come to terms with your emotions, schedule a meeting with your boss and with your Human Resources representative. While restating your commitment to continued success in your current position, the team and company goals, and your own career advancement, ask questions requiring a specific answer:

- "What do you think I can learn or demonstrate that will prepare me for the next promotional opportunity?" Look for both technical and behavioral answers, and be careful not to challenge at this point. If your boss mentions that you came up short on a skill that you believe you've mastered, then your boss has not see you demonstrate this skill (a visibility issue). Review these answers against your Results Profile for the target position, and prepare to redesign your self-promotion plan (Chapter 8) or your rebound plan (Chapter 1).

- "Do you believe that I am suited—or ready—for this type of promotion? If not, why not?" This is not a debate in defense of your position; this is a forum for collecting information. Take notes, ask for clarification or examples if appropriate—and leave it there. If your boss or the Human Resources representative has the perception that you are not suited or ready for a promotion, arguing the point now will not help. Take the information, and decide whether a rebound plan is in order or whether it is time to move on (and out).

Before you leave the meeting, request more challenging (and visible) assignments in your current job in preparation for your future. In closing, commit to preparing a personal development plan, and ask your boss or the Human Resources representative to review it with you to make sure that your path and the direction of the company are synchronized.

After your meeting, send an email thank-you to your boss or the HR rep, and set a date for the follow-up development plan review meeting. Have another look at self-promotion (Chapter 8), and create a plan that will work toward the goals you and your boss have set, maintaining a high level of accurate, positive visibility.

Final Thoughts on Getting a Promotion

Your career is your responsibility, and asking for a promotion is the true test of taking control of your career. If you did not get the promotion you wanted, something is missing for you, for your company, or both. If, after seeking honest and meaningful feedback, you find there is something you can learn, commit to learning it. If there is a cultural or political mismatch, think about moving on by moving out of your current company. Do not leave the management of your career to someone else—or to chance. Take control and be ready for the next opportunity.

Concepts to Remember

1. Make it easy for your boss to promote you.

2. Do your best, and make sure that your best is exactly what is needed.

3. Evaluate how you are seen by others.

4. Plan to move toward your goal, not simply away from a job you don't like.

5. Define your objective for your career.

6. Prepare, then take action: Ask for the promotion.

7. If you asked, but were denied a promotion, analyze, regroup, and move on—you are in control of your own career.

PART 3

MOVING ON

"Parting is such sweet sorrow . . ."

Well, in matters of love, yes. In matters of work, parting can range from exciting to devastating, depending on who made the decision that it was time for you to move on.

Taking control of your career includes developing your own crystal ball of sorts—significantly increasing your level of awareness, paying more attention to your inklings about what is going on inside of you and around you, and choosing how you want things to turn out. The following examples give you a sense of the level of control you have over the decisions you make and the risks you take when you leave a job.

Nancy's story:

For 3 years, Nancy had arrived at her office every day with her mind in turmoil and a chip on her shoulder. She was going through a protracted divorce, and the last thing she needed was for her boss, Paul, to make another stupid, time-consuming error in booking an event—a mistake that she would have to fix.

This was the last straw. Paul had booked a wedding at the facility some 6 months previously and had told no one. He had forgotten to write it down, he had forgotten to arrange for the flowers, he had forgotten to arrange for the extra chairs, he had forgotten to arrange for the parking attendants, he had forgotten to get an insurance binder—he had forgotten everything. On this day, the bride and groom showed up at noon with 150 of their closest friends: no flowers, no chairs, no nothing.

When Paul arrived at the center at Nancy's urgent request that final day, he blamed everyone for his mistake—everyone but himself. Nancy had had enough; she walked out.

At 55, Nancy found herself newly single, unemployed, and scared to death.

Steve's story:

Steve had been a patent attorney for 17 years. He went to law school because his father wanted him to go to law school, and he became a patent attorney because his father wanted him to become a patent attorney. He married, had two children, lived in a large house they could barely afford, drove expensive cars, and had an enormous amount of debt. To the outside world, Steve had the perfect lifestyle; on the inside, he was miserable living the life his father had always wanted.

Just after his fortieth birthday, Steve decided that he wanted to ratchet down his lifestyle, so without giving much *thought to his values or where he wanted to be, he quickly got away from what he thought was making him crazy—he quit his job and became an eighth-grade history teacher.*

After 5 months, Steve realized that he had made a huge mistake, and he had never been so scared or unhappy.

Tim's story:

In August, Tim began a new job as VP of information technology in a San Francisco–based telecommunications firm. In September, the CEO, to whom Tim reported, unexpectedly quit. When the new CEO was brought in, Tim immediately knew that he had a challenge on his hands: This guy was tough, abrupt, and intimidating in his approach to his leadership team.

In early January, Tim noticed that his subordinate, James, was having weekly luncheon meetings with the CEO, yet Tim said nothing.

In March, the CEO asked Tim to review a PowerPoint presentation he had prepared to deliver to the board of directors—page 14 of which indicated that Tim should be replaced, as he was ineffective. Tim dutifully reviewed the PowerPoint presentation and said nothing.

In April, Tim was terminated and replaced by his subordinate, James. He was offered no package; he was given 2 weeks' severance and shown the door.

Anne's story:

In the months after the terrorist attacks in New York City, Anne gave a lot of thought to her career, her life, and her vision for her future. At 42, she was happily single and working as a sen-

ior marketing executive for a Fortune 500 company based in Manhattan. She had great friends, a great home, and a great job—yet something was missing. She hired me as her coach to help her find "it."

We worked together to evaluate her life-balance status, to uncover her values, and to identify, eliminate, or leverage her needs. Although she had started her career in broadcast entertainment marketing in Los Angeles, she had been sidetracked by the terrific Manhattan opportunity. She realized that she was good at working as a senior marketing executive, and that she enjoyed most of her work there, yet the job did not use some of her talents and strengths that were important to her. Her coaching work helped her to put a name to the gap she had sensed; she knew exactly who she was, exactly what was missing, and exactly where she wanted to be going forward.

Anne planned her departure from her Manhattan position, arranged her finances to allow for a long-distance and possibly lengthy job hunt, planned and negotiated an exit strategy, and gave her employer 30 days' notice. With a glowing reference, a targeted plan to get a job with one of the companies she admired, and a huge amount of courage, she began working at the job of getting a job.

Four months later, Anne landed a plum position with a major studio as vice president of marketing. She sold her East Coast home and purchased a new home in Los Angeles in the same area in which she grew up. She was closer to her family, she had found a job she loved, she was making more money, and she was having more fun. And she has never been happier.

Nancy, Steve, Tim, and Anne each realized that it was time to move on, yet each handled it differently: One departed in anger, one departed on a whim, one was in denial, and one made a plan and worked it. Each had the option of controlling what happened next, yet each experienced a different outcome.

Not every departure is as seamless as Anne's. There are also the "not in my control" possibilities of separation or termination, including

1. You are ethical; your boss, the CFO, is not. You refuse to cook the books, and your employment is terminated.

2. Your skills are out of date; technology has passed you by, you have ignored requests to upgrade your skills, and your employer is tired of asking you to learn.

3. You are known to be difficult, pushy, abusive, and abrasive, and you have destroyed your reputation to the point of no return. You figured that you would have a lengthy run at this company because it needed your expertise so desperately. However, your employer finds it easier to ask you to leave than to continue to ask you to change, and you are shown the door.

4. Your relationship with your boss has been irretrievably damaged, and your rebound plan has not worked. With fear and trepidation about your reaction, your employer cuts you loose.

5. The company is in a fatal downward spiral, and while there have been no announcements, you know that it will not last another quarter.

6. The company has auditors in, completing due diligence in preparation for your firm's purchase by a larger concern.

7. You have been "layered" (someone has been slipped into a position between you and your boss, effectively giving you a demotion).

Whichever your exit situation, you still have control of your next steps, which can make the difference between taking the *first* thing that comes your way and taking the *best* thing that you uncover. It is also the difference between encountering the same stifling workplace experiences yet again and finding the job that exactly fits your style, your skills, your values, and your vision for a life you love.

The following chapters outline a plan that you can use when it is time for you to move on—whether it is your decision or not.

If, When, and How to Leave Your Job

> *The definition of insanity is doing the same thing again and again and expecting a different result.*
> —*Albert Einstein*

There comes a time in every career when you question whether it makes sense to continue or not.

At one point in my corporate career, I was reporting to a man whose behavior vacillated between "Kindly Southern Gentleman" and "Wacko Hostile-man." He could be soft-spoken and charming one moment, and then scream, throw things, and disparage you the next—and there was no way of telling which of these behavioral styles you were going to encounter at any given moment.

As I was a remote employee, it took me a little time to catch on—and while I certainly was not his only target, I was apparently one of his favorite targets. Each meeting I attended in the company's headquarters offices allowed me to see the mask of civility displayed in the interview process melt away. Moreover, the untargeted members of the management team followed his lead, and they often played right along with the office politics surrounding this antagonistic and often discriminatory behavior.

I created and implemented a plan to set some boundaries around how I would be treated, what kinds of jokes I thought were inappropriate, and what tone of voice would work for me, and I asked for the support of Human Resources management. As sometimes happens, this boss was a long-term employee, and while Human Resources agreed that his behavior was offensive, they made it clear that they were willing to look the other way.

I was not. There was no way this was going to work for me. After only 5 months of employment with this organization, I knew it was time to leave. I submitted my resignation, we developed a mutually beneficial transition plan, and I moved on.

It was the smartest thing I ever did.

When All Else Fails

There is never really a good time to quit your job in a huff, even though some workplace nonsense can make you crazy enough to do just that. With a focus on preparation rather than paranoia, what are the clues or signals that it is time for you to move on?

You may be ready to move on if

1. You dislike your boss or your boss dislikes you, and you cannot resolve this.

2. You have a conflict with a peer, subordinate, or customer (internal or external), and you have been unable to work it out.

3. You do not enjoy the work you do, and no amount of vacationing will fix it.

4. You are in full-blown burnout and suffering the physical symptoms of stress, including headaches, sleeplessness, anxiety, or depression.

5. Key individuals in your organization lack integrity, and you cannot justify their actions any longer.

6. Your work environment is chaotic, verbally abusive, hostile, disrespectful, or demeaning.

7. You no longer feel that your contribution is appreciated—something is wrong, and you cannot put your finger on it.

8. Your work is constantly criticized—or ignored.

9. You are known in your organization as difficult and aggressive.

10. You have made a workplace or political blunder, and your rebound plan has not worked.

11. You have applied for a promotion, and the reasons for your being rejected are flimsy at best.

12. You have been "layered"—that is, your boss has hired someone to manage you (you report to the new guy, and the new guy reports to your boss).

13. You have attempted to develop a mentor relationship with members of management, but you have been avoided or turned down.

14. You have not improved your career skills within the last 90 days.

15. You have been overlooked for important meetings, task forces, and initiatives.

16. Your last performance evaluation recommended skill or behavior enhancements for you to master, and you have neglected to do so.

17. Your company is in merger talks with another company or your company is in financial trouble.

18. Your boss has been fired (or has left to pursue other opportunities), and you are guilty by association.

19. Your company has hired a new CEO, and he has begun to hire his own leadership team.

20. You are elated on Friday afternoons and depressed on Sunday nights.

If you agreed with seven or more of these statements, you will want to either take some steps to stabilize your current position (refer back to Chapters 1 to 5) or plan your exit.

Planning for When and How

Nancy, the woman who was going through a nasty divorce and had to deal with an incompetent boss, reacted out of anger, and it did not serve her well. She removed herself from a frustrating situation by abruptly quitting; she was clearly running *away* from something rather than being drawn *toward* something better.

If you find yourself in a similarly frustrating situation, ask yourself the following questions:

1. How did I get here?

2. Have I experienced this before?

3. What part of this relationship can I own and shift?

4. What are my options?

5. How do I want this to turn out?

Steve, the patent attorney who became a history teacher, had good intentions in his desire to separate, but he did not investigate why being an attorney wasn't working for him any longer, and what it was about teaching that would give him what he wanted. Steve could have asked himself the following questions:

1. What was most satisfying in being an attorney?

2. What was most dissatisfying?

3. How do those things fit (or contrast) with my values?

4. What needs were fulfilled by following my father's expectations, and how are those actions serving me now? What values and needs do I have now?

5. How can I take my skills and my values, and create a balanced life that I love?

Tim, our IT person who was replaced by his own subordinate, received many clues about his job stability—clues that he chose to ignore (doing nothing is a choice). He did not ask

1. What type of management support do I need in order to be effective and productive in this job?

2. How can the new CEO support me as I work to deliver the results he wants? How can we best communicate with each other?

3. What about the meetings between my subordinate and my boss? If the CEO is *mentoring* my subordinate, how can I support the process? If the CEO is *grooming* my subordinate, what are the chances for my success here?

4. What about the PowerPoint recommendation for my removal? If he believes I am ineffective, why is this? Can a strategy be implemented to turn this around, or is it over for me?

5. Since the clues and discussions all point to my departure, what is the best process to use to leave, and how can I ensure that I do not experience this again?

Anne's departure was easy because it was her choice, yet it was difficult because it required an enormous amount of courage. Working with me as her coach, Anne took the time to learn what she wanted before she departed, and she is now happy and balanced in her life and her career. She answered her questions about who she was and what she wanted, and then implemented her strategy to get it. You can use her plan as a template for your own strategy, including pre-work (covered in Chapters 1 to 5) and implementation. First, her pre-work:

- *Discovery:* Determine values and needs.

- *Identification:* Determine job satisfiers and dissatisfiers; compare to values and needs.

- *Research:* Can she apply her strengths and skills and honor her values in her current organization?

- *Development:* Prepare vision and mission statement, set goals.

- *Decisions:* What types of positions would suit her, and in what industries?

- *Assessment:* Could she be comfortable without an income, and for how long? If an ongoing income is required, how much time could she spend on her job hunt while she was still employed? (*Note:* If you look for work while you are still working, you still have to deliver results!)

Next, Anne implemented her strategy. Her plan included the following steps.

Negotiating an Exit Package   Since Anne had a great relationship with her boss, negotiating her exit package was comfortable. Her boss had been an active participant in Anne's research concerning her desire to move ahead in her career, so her departure, while disappointing to him, came as no surprise.

In exchange for 30 days' notice and a transition plan to integrate a new person into Anne's role, she received an extra 4 weeks' pay. When this was added to the 10 weeks' vacation she had accrued and the departure package that was given to all senior executives (another 6 months' pay), Anne was able to leave her job with more than 9 months' salary, continued insurance coverage, and options to exercise. She was also entitled to a raise during her notice period, which the company allowed! (It is not often that one gets a raise when one is leaving a job.)

If you find yourself working with a great boss in a job that is not right, take a lesson from Anne: Work with your boss to figure it out. If you and your boss do not have a healthy relationship, you may approach the collaboration process differently.

Put It in Writing   Many people must negotiate an exit package in uncomfortable circumstances. However, even in the worst-case scenarios, it is never wise to articulate your anger and frustration in your letter of resignation. An unheated discussion with your boss, followed by a simple letter of resignation and the outline of an exit plan, is the way to go.

Depending on your position and the length of the notice you give (knowing that most employers will escort you to the door the minute you give your notice), your exit plan will serve as your compass during your transition. Consider the following:

1. Are you entitled to accrued vacation or severance?

2. Will your title and salary remain constant during the transition and severance period?

3. Will you receive a lump-sum severance payment on the day you leave, or will you receive salary continuation?

4. If you will receive salary continuation, will payment cease upon your acceptance of new employment?

5. Will you be free to take time off for personal business during the transitional period?

6. Will your benefits continue during both the transitional and the severance period?

7. Are you entitled to any bonuses (profit sharing, incentives, or other bonuses paid at target achievement level) during the severance period as though you were a full-time employee?

8. How will existing stock options be handled?

9. What type of written or verbal reference statement will be delivered to your prospective employers regarding the circumstances of your departure? Develop a mutually agreed-upon letter of reference or statement to be used.

It is important to note that any termination of employment that is in violation of Title VII (discrimination) may require the attention of an attorney. See Chapter 15 for references.

The exit package you negotiate must be fair to both parties.

This is not an opportunity for retribution, no matter how angry you are! Let this negotiation represent a sound basis for a smooth transition.

Five Tips for Getting Over a Job Loss

Many people—professionals and executives—find that they must move forward in their career search with a positive spin on what feels like a negative situation. The following five tips are most important in getting through this process quickly, and intact.

1. *Allow time to grieve, but do not dwell there.* Losing your job is a stressful event, and if you define yourself by what you do, leaving that job (voluntarily or involuntarily) is particularly stressful. You may lose your sense of self-worth, and that will be a barrier to moving forward.

    When you have been given your marching orders, the first thing to do is to realize that, in the words of *The Godfather,* "It's not personal, it's just business." As personal as a job loss may seem to you, being terminated or laid off is simply representative of a shift in how your organization wants to run its business. Rather than looking for someone to blame (including yourself), you need to realize that you are the same knowledgeable, experienced, and effective person that you were before your job disappeared.

    Even so, a job loss is like any other loss: You will need time to adjust, and you may need emotional support or therapy to work through the stages of grief (denial, anxiety, depression, anger, guilt, and acceptance). Allow yourself time to grieve for your loss, learn the lessons associated with your loss, and work toward acceptance of the situation. When you are stuck in the anxiety-depression-anger-guilt section of the grieving process, it shows in everything you do—your interviews, your networking, and your cover letters. Get help if you need it so that you can heal and move through it, and move on.

2. *Get your financial house in order.* Now is a good time to get a handle on the practical side of your life—what financial resources you currently have, what resources your employer will provide (severance pay, outplacement, and so on), and what financial benefits may be available through the Employment Department of your state. Also, make sure you take care of your health insurance coverage (COBRA allows you to purchase health coverage at the group rate, but an application deadline applies, so do this early). Take care of yourself by taking care of the money.

3. *Become a career activist.* Activism is any practice that emphasizes direct and vigorous action, especially in support of (or opposition to) one side of a controversial issue. I'm a product of the 1960s, so activism is in my blood.

When you are in active career transition, you can use that same energy to become a career activist, that is, you can use direct and vigorous action to take control of your own career choices. Using your knowledge of yourself, your values, your skills, and your strengths as a foundation, your career activism will make you the chief executive officer, chief marketing officer, and chief sales officer of the "Get Me a Job" company. In these roles, you will be taking direct action and making the decisions that will get you what you want in your next job. You are in charge of what happens next, so being a career activist means that you are taking responsibility for your life and career, and taking the actions that are required to make your next move your best move.

4. *Manage your time.* Career transition is not a time to slack off, but it is not a time to overwork, either. If you are in active career transition (not employed elsewhere), plan on working 30 to 40 hours each week on your job search plan. If you are currently employed and making the transition out, plan on at least 10 to 15 hours of work each week on your job search plan.

   When people are in transition, they are often so focused on what they need (a job) that they forget to take good care of themselves. Build a self-care regime into your time management system by taking time every day to do something that is fun and non-job-related (and within your financial means). This could be a walk or bike ride, a movie, or a good book—whatever it takes to give you some "regrouping" time.

5. *Balance your life.* A balanced life means a healthy, happy, productive you, with solid relationships, financial security, a job you love, and a spirit that is nourished. It is possible to have a life that is filled with balance, even in a time of career transition.

   Think about each of these categories of life balance as a silo to be filled and maintained—including a reserve of about 10 percent more than you need. That way, if your job disappears, you still have healthy and supportive relationships, finances in reserve, and a spirit that is nourished, and you are healthy; all you need to do is find a job you love to fit into your balanced life.

A balanced life is not a pie-in-the-sky dream; it is real, and you can have it. Once you identify your current life-balance status, you can work to build reserves in each area (even during a job search campaign). Take the Coach U assessment, Clean Sweep (Exhibit 13-1) to get a sense of your life balance, and take action to balance your life.

The first time I took the Clean Sweep assessment, I scored 37 out of 100! I was in a job I did not like, I had unhealthy relationships, my finances were a mess, I was physically unhealthy, and I had no sense of my spirit (my core, my purpose here on Earth, my direction). Taking that assessment was a life-changer for me. I quickly learned what shifts I had to make in my life in order to create the balance I wanted while building a life and a career that I love.

Final Thoughts on Leaving Your Job

Sometimes we know that it is time to go, but we deny it (I have done this myself). Sometimes we know that it is time to go, but we fight it (I have done this, too). Sometimes we do not know that it is time to go, and we are caught unawares (I have experienced this, too). The best cases are those in which you know, plan, and take action to control your own career.

Exhibit 13-1

Clean Sweep Program

You have more natural energy when you are clear with your environment, health and emotional balance, money and relationships.

The **Clean Sweep** Program consists of 100 items which, when completed, give you the vitality and strength you want.

The program can be completed in less than one year.

INSTRUCTIONS

There are 4 steps to completing the **Clean Sweep™ Program.**

Step 1: Answer each question. If true, check the box. Be rigorous; be a hard grader. If the statement is sometimes or usually true please DO NOT check the box until the statement is virtually always true for you. (No "credit" until it is really true!) If the statement does not apply to you, check the box. If the statement will never be true for you, check the box. (You get "credit" for it because it does not apply or will never happen.) And, you may change any statement to fit your situation better.

Step 2: Summarize each section. Add up the number of True boxes for each of the 4 sections and write those amounts where indicated. Then add up all four sections and write the current total in the box on the front of this form.

Step 3: Color in the Progress Chart on the front page. Always start from the bottom up. The goal is to have the entire chart filled in. In the meantime, you will have a current picture of how you are doing in each of the four areas.

Step 4: Keep playing until all boxes are filled in. You can do it! This process may take 30 or 360 days, but you can achieve a Clean Sweep! Use your coach or a friend to assist you. And check back once a year for maintenance.

PROGRESS CHART

Date	Points (+/-)	Score

CLEAN SWEEP PROGRAM
100-POINT CHECKLIST

#	\multicolumn{4}{Sections}
	A	B	C	D
25				
24				
23				
22				
21				
20				
19				
18				
17				
16				
15				
14				
13				
12				
11				
10				
9				
8				
7				
6				
5				
4				
3				
2				
1				

Give yourself credit as you get points from the 100-point program. Fill in columns from the bottom up.

A. PHYSICAL ENVIRONMENT

- ☐ My personal files, papers and receipts are neatly filed away.
- ☐ My car is in excellent condition. (Doesn't need mechanical work, repairs, cleaning or replacing)
- ☐ My home is neat and clean. (Vacuumed, closets clean, desks and tables clear, furniture in good repair; windows clean)
- ☐ My appliances, machinery and equipment work well. (Refrigerator, toaster, snow-blower, water heater, toys)
- ☐ My clothes are all pressed, clean and make me look great. (No wrinkles, baskets of laundry, torn, out-of-date or ill-fitting clothes)
- ☐ My plants and animals are healthy. (Fed, watered, getting light and love)
- ☐ My bed/bedroom lets me have the best sleep possible. (Firm bed, light, air)
- ☐ I live in a home/apartment that I love.
- ☐ I surround myself with beautiful things.
- ☐ I live in the geographic area I choose.
- ☐ There is ample and healthy light around me.
- ☐ I consistently have adequate time, space and freedom in my life.
- ☐ I am not damaged by my environment.
- ☐ I am not tolerating anything about my home or work environment.
- ☐ My work environment is productive and inspiring. (Synergistic, ample tools and resources; no undue pressure)
- ☐ I recycle.
- ☐ I use non ozone-depleting products.
- ☐ My hair is the way I want it.
- ☐ I surround myself with music, which makes my life more enjoyable.
- ☐ My bed is made daily.
- ☐ I don't injure myself, or bump into things.
- ☐ People feel comfortable in my home.
- ☐ I drink purified water.
- ☐ I have nothing around the house or in storage that I do not need.
- ☐ I am consistently early or easily on time.

___ **Number of boxes checked (25 max)**

B. HEALTH & EMOTIONAL BALANCE

- ☐ I rarely use caffeine. (Chocolate, coffee, colas, tea) less than 3 times per week, total.
- ☐ I rarely eat sugar. (Less than 3 times per week.)
- ☐ I rarely watch television. (Less than 5 hours per week)
- ☐ I rarely drink alcohol. (Less than 2 drinks per week)
- ☐ My teeth and gums are healthy. (Have seen dentist in last 6 months)
- ☐ My cholesterol count is healthful.
- ☐ My blood pressure is healthful.
- ☐ I have had a complete physical exam in the past 3 years.
- ☐ I do not smoke tobacco or other substances.
- ☐ I do not use illegal drugs or misuse prescribed medications.
- ☐ I have had a complete eye exam within the past two years. (Glaucoma check, vision test)
- ☐ My weight is within my ideal range.
- ☐ My nails are healthy and attractive.
- ☐ I don't rush or use adrenaline to get the job done.
- ☐ I have a rewarding life beyond my work or profession.
- ☐ I have something to look forward to virtually every day.
- ☐ I have no habits that I find to be unacceptable.
- ☐ I am aware of the physical or emotional problems or conditions I have, and I am now fully taking care of all of them.
- ☐ I consistently take evenings, weekends and holidays off and take at least two weeks of vacation each year.
- ☐ I have been tested for the AIDS antibody.
- ☐ I use well-made sunglasses.
- ☐ I do not suffer.
- ☐ I floss daily.
- ☐ I walk or exercise at least three times per week.
- ☐ I hear well.

___ **Number of boxes checked (25 max)**

c. MONEY

- ☐ I currently save at least 10% of my income.
- ☐ I pay my bills on time, virtually always.
- ☐ My income source/revenue base is stable and predictable.
- ☐ I know how much I must have to be minimally financially independent and I have a plan to get there.
- ☐ I have returned or made-good-on any money I borrowed.
- ☐ I have written agreements and am current with payments to individuals or companies to whom I owe money.
- ☐ I have 6 months' living expenses in a money market-type account.
- ☐ I live on a weekly budget that allows me to save and not suffer.
- ☐ All my tax returns have been filed and all my taxes have been paid.
- ☐ I currently live well, within my means.
- ☐ I have excellent medical insurance.
- ☐ My assets (car, home, possessions, treasures) are well insured.
- ☐ I have a financial plan for the next year.
- ☐ I have no legal clouds hanging over me.
- ☐ My will is up-to-date and accurate.
- ☐ Any parking tickets, alimony or child supports are paid and current.
- ☐ My investments do not keep me awake at night.
- ☐ I know how much I am worth.
- ☐ I am on a career/professional/business track that is or will soon be financially and personally rewarding.
- ☐ My earnings are commensurate with the effort I put into my job.
- ☐ I have no "loose ends" at work.
- ☐ I am in relationship with people who can assist in my career/professional development.
- ☐ I rarely miss work due to illness.
- ☐ I am putting aside enough money each month to reach financial independence.
- ☐ My earnings outpace inflation, consistently.

____   **Number of boxes checked (25 max)**

d. RELATIONSHIPS

- ☐ I have told my parents, in the last 3 months, that I love them.
- ☐ I get along well with my sibling(s).
- ☐ I get along well with my co-workers/clients.
- ☐ I get along well with my manager/staff.
- ☐ There is no one who I would dread or feel uncomfortable "running across". (In the street, at an airport or party)
- ☐ I put people first and results second.
- ☐ I have let go of the relationships that drag me down or damage me. ("Let go" means to end, walk away from, state, handle, no longer be attached to)
- ☐ I have communicated or attempted to communicate with everyone who I have damaged, injured or seriously disturbed, even if it wasn't fully my fault.
- ☐ I do not gossip or talk about others.
- ☐ I have a circle of friends/family who love and appreciate me for who I am, more than just what I do for them.
- ☐ I tell people how they can satisfy me.
- ☐ I am fully caught up with letters and calls.
- ☐ I always tell the truth, no matter what.
- ☐ I receive enough love from people around me to feel good.
- ☐ I have fully forgiven those people who have hurt/damaged me, deliberate or not.
- ☐ I am a person of his/her word; people can count on me.
- ☐ I quickly clear miscommunications and misunderstandings when they do occur.
- ☐ I live life on my terms, not by the rules or preferences of others.
- ☐ There is nothing unresolved with past loves or spouses.
- ☐ I am in tune with my wants and needs and get them taken care of.
- ☐ I do not judge or criticize others.
- ☐ I do not "take personally" the things that people say to me.
- ☐ I have a best friend or soul mate.
- ☐ I state requirements rather than complain.
- ☐ I spend time with people who don't try to change me.

____   **Number of boxes checked (25 max)**

BENEFITS

On the lines below, jot down specific benefits, results and shifts that happen in your life because you handled an item in the **Clean Sweep** Program.

Date   Benefit

_____
_____
_____
_____
_____
_____
_____
_____

INTELLECTUAL PROPERTY NOTICE

From my own experience, as well as the experiences of my clients, I have found that leaving a job takes as much work as finding a job. Deciding if, when, and how to leave is much easier when you are in touch with both what is going on inside of your organization and what is going on inside of *you*. This awareness gives you more options, *earlier*—and a sense of control that cannot get any other way.

Concepts to Remember

1. Be aware of the clues and signals that it is time to move on.

2. Make a plan for your departure, with integrity.

3. Prepare, then take action.

4. Take the time you need to grieve for your job loss, then move on.

5. Deal with the financial aspects of your job loss.

6. Practice career activism: Take direct and vigorous action.

7. Manage your time.

8. Balance your life: relationships, health, finances, environment, and spirit.

14

The Rules of the Road to
a New Career

Kathleen, like most people who are in a career transition, wants this process to end. She wants a job, and the sooner, the better. Not particularly extroverted, this finance manager is hoping that she will find something quickly through Internet job boards.

She spends hours each day searching the Internet and responding to postings. Some of them sound like a perfect fit; others sound a little less perfect, but she would take anything that was remotely close at this point.

After several weeks, she has not received one interview request—nor has she heard anything from any of the 100 résumés she has sent out. She has also called a number of executive recruiters, with no success—no interviews, no offers, no job.

Who Is in Control Here?

Taking control of your job search means that you shift your focus from waiting for a job to come along that sounds right to conducting a search for a job that is right. It means that you take control of where you look and what you look for, in an effort to find that right fit. It means that you are less inclined to be disappointed by the lack of response to your efforts and more inclined to decide where you want to work and how you want to fit in there. It also means that you will be tapping into the unpublished job market—a process that goes far beyond searching the job boards.

The Unpublished Job Market

According to the U.S. Department of Labor, the job market can be divided into two categories:

1. The formal, published job market. These jobs are typically publicized through newspaper advertisements, recruiting agencies, and job boards. This formal, published job market constitutes about 25 percent of the available jobs.

2. The informal or unpublished job market. This includes those job openings that are filled *without* being advertised.

To access the *unpublished* job market, representing about 75 percent of the total job market, you have to network (see the discussion in item 4, of the next section).

For an example of how you can tap into that unpublished

job market, take Brett's case. (The story of Brett's boss taking credit for Brett's work was described in Chapter 2.) Brett is a life-long networker: He attended industry events, conventions, and educational seminars, and he consistently attended our Los Angeles Executive Networking Roundtable meetings (see Chapter 15 for a link to more information on these meetings). Brett made a point of getting to know the others in the room, and he worked to develop relationships with the people he met.

During one of our meetings, Brett met Gary, another executive who was developing a network to land his next position. Gary had been a CFO, and he was interested in trying to go in a new direction by purchasing a franchise. His requirements were simple: that the franchise operation be financially healthy, that it be close to home, and that it involve his long-time passion: cars.

As Brett and Gary shared information about what they each wanted, they talked about how they could help each other. Gary mentioned that a friend of his, the CEO of a Los Angeles–based diversified services company, was looking for a new general manager to run day-to-day operations and oversee the firm's West Coast operations. Brett knew of the company; in fact, he had already targeted it as one that he would like to learn more about as a possible next step in his career. Brett asked if Gary could arrange an introduction to the CEO; a luncheon meeting was held, then a dinner meeting—-and within 2 weeks, Brett received a job offer. The job had not been published. Gary was aware of it only because his friend had mentioned it.

As it turned out, Brett's brother owned a franchise that he was interested in selling. The franchise, an upscale automotive repair and maintenance shop, was just what Gary wanted: automotive-based and close to home. Gary made an offer to purchase; Brett's brother accepted.

Mastering the Routes to a New Career

Regardless of your means of entry into the career transition process, there are four well-known paths to landing a new job:

1. Responding to job postings

2. Direct mail campaigns

3. Executive recruiters, employment agencies, and search firms

4. Networking

Each of these four methods is an important piece of a great job search campaign, but some have a bigger return on investment (ROI) than others. First, let's review each component.

1. *Responding to postings.* This is usually the first order of business for someone in transition. Most people consider responding to Internet postings to be the updated version of checking the newspaper want ads. Although it is not the most effective job-hunting method, responding to job postings is relatively easy: You point your browser at your favorite job listing web site, apply a few filters, and review the list of jobs that match your criteria.

   The good news is that there are plenty of jobs listed; the bad news is that many of those jobs may be dated, and you may not receive any reply to your application. About 10 percent of job hunters find their next assignments through this process, so spending some of your job-hunting time searching the job boards is wise; spending too much time doing this is counterproductive.

2. *Direct mail campaigns.* This is another relatively easy process. A good direct mail campaign starts with a target list of companies, a great résumé, and a cover letter that you can alter for each situation. If you prepare a direct mail campaign yourself, your direct expenses will include paper, printing, and postage, and your indirect expenses will include the time involved in researching the companies to target. It is important to know that you should expect one interview (with a hiring manager, not a Human Resources representative or recruiter) for every 1000 unsolicited résumés you send out. That makes the direct mail process the least productive of the standard job search techniques.

3. *Executive recruiters, employment agencies, and search firms.* About 10 percent of job seekers find their next assignment through recruiters and search firms. Even so, finding the right recruiter can increase your chances of success. There are several separate and distinct categories of recruiters, and it is important for you to know the difference.

   Executive recruiters represent the *employer*. They are specialists, and they do a great deal of research to find the best three or four candidates, whom they present to an employer for placement. They are paid a higher fee than agencies, and most of them are engaged on a "retainer" basis, that is, they are paid a fee whether or not the candidates they present are hired. Retained executive recruiters rarely advertise, since they most often present candidates who are not currently looking for employment (that is, they present only people who are currently employed). This may mean that those people who are in active career transition (unemployed) will not be considered for any of their opportunities.

Another category of executive recruiter is the "contingent" variety. A contingent recruiter receives a fee only if the candidate the recruiter supplies is hired. Again, contingent recruiters represent the *employer*, not the candidate, and they typically send several candidates to the employer for one opening in an attempt to ensure that one of their candidates will be selected to fill the opening.

Employment agencies or search firms usually handle positions with salaries of less than $50,000 per year. Typically specialized, these agencies may handle HR, finance, administrative support, or clerical positions. Again, employment agencies and search firms represent the *employer*, not the job seeker. They probably will show interest in you only when they know of a specific opportunity that calls for someone with your background and experience.

Working with recruiters can be helpful, or it can be a waste of time. You can control your level of success in using them by conducting research (see Chapter 15 for a link to research recommendations). The following 10 rules apply to working with recruiters:

- Be honest with yourself about your skills, education, background, and career path, and then be honest with the recruiter.

- Do your homework on the recruiter. Make sure you know, understand, and respect the recruiter's business model (retained or contingent) and industry specialty.
- Do some preparatory work before your initial telephone interview with the recruiter. Be prepared for the standard questions, and prepare a few examples of your experience to support your case. Also be prepared for that one question you do not want to have to answer (it will be asked!).
- Be ready to respond immediately. If the recruiter has lined up an interview for you, make yourself available.
- Do not call the recruiter daily or weekly. Ask the recruiter what an appropriate follow-up schedule for the two of you to touch base might be, and then respect that.
- Make sure the recruiter knows how you like to receive feedback after interviews—timing, content, and style. If the recruiter indicates that he or she cannot provide the type of feedback you find important, you have selected the wrong recruiter.
- Know what you want, and be able to communicate it clearly to the recruiter. It is very easy for job hunters to appear ambivalent about their direction when they really just want to be open to all possibilities.
- Be helpful. If you are not interested in a position that is suggested to you, make sure that the recruiter understands why you think the suggested position is not a good fit, and offer to recommend

people you know who you believe will be a good
fit.

- Good recruiters receive hundreds of résumés each
week; they will not respond to every résumé they
receive. They will respond to you if they know you
or if they know the person who referred you to
them, and they will respond to you when they have
an actual opportunity that would be a good fit.
- Remember that the recruiter works for the
employer.

Responding to job postings, working with executive recruiters, and engaging in direct mail campaigns
are important components of an effective job search,
but you get the biggest return on your investment
through networking.

4. *Networking.* If you have experienced the frustration of
waiting for the right job to show up on Internet postings, you will be pleased to find that real results occur
when you take control of your own career. Networking
is not as dreadful as you may think. It is not a process
of stalking someone—it is a process of developing relationships that last, it is a process of making contacts
that may have information for you (and with whom
you may be able to reciprocate), and it is a path to the
research on target companies that you will be doing
during your search.

If it is true that over 75 percent of all jobs are found
through word of mouth, then networking is an important element of finding the work you love. That would
also mean that 75 percent of your job search time would
best be spent in the networking arena.

- Networking is
  - A way to develop important, long-lasting relationships
  - A way to research information on industries, companies, cultures, and jobs
  - A way to be helpful to others
  - A way to restore the sense of "team" that is missing from your day-to-day activities when you are in a career transition
  - A primary source of unpublished jobs
  - Fun
- Networking is *not*
  - Simply asking someone for a job
  - An excuse to market a product or service
  - An excuse to stalk someone

A solid network is something that we each need, whether we are in transition or in a job we love, and a network is easiest to develop when you do not need it. If you have let your network slip, work to rebuild it and keep it healthy. The members of your network will benefit from your expertise and contacts as much as you will benefit from theirs.

How to Build a Network If you were to ask 30 people you know for advice in your job search, and each of them referred you to 3 other people who might be able to assist you in some way, and each of those people, in turn, referred you to 3 additional people, you would have a network of three levels of people with 270 contacts involved in supporting your job search.

Networking is most productive and fun when it is done in person (although it can be done via the Internet and Usenet groups). I recommend that my clients attend networking meetings in their area that focus on their target audience, from executive to entry-level groups. Try out a couple of groups and meetings before you make any long-term or financial commitments; you have to be comfortable with the group and its charter first.

In the networking meetings for professionals and executives in a career transition that I facilitate here in California, each participant is requested to come to the meetings with three things in mind:

1. *An elevator speech.* This is your short answer to the "tell me about yourself" question: In about 30-seconds, describe yourself, your background, and your direction. Consider the following questions when creating your elevator speech:
   - Who are you?
   - What is your specialty (or product, or service)?
   - What problem does your service solve, or what value does it add?
   An example is

   "My name is John Doe, and I am a seasoned operations management professional with experience in manufacturing and food and beverage. I help companies keep their operations running smoothly, while increasing productivity and revenue."

2. *What they want to get from the group before they leave.* Often people attend networking meetings and say something like, "I'm looking for a CFO job." Where? What industry? What type of corporate culture? What size company? Be specific in articulating your direction:

"I am in a career transition, and I'd like to meet contacts with Dole, Del Monte, Campbell's, and Nestlé, so if any of you have contacts in these companies, I'd love to spend a few minutes with you today after this meeting, or I can be reached via email at abc@xyz.com."

3. *Something to share.* You know many people who will be helpful to others in their job search campaign, so offering to assist someone else by providing an introduction is valuable. Just do not share any contacts that you know will be unwilling to participate, or that are virtually unknown to you.

How to Work with Your Network

1. *Categorize.* Make a point of creating a database of the people you meet and those you already know. For instance, categories within your network could be your closest friends and allies (centers of influence), your coworkers, your clients, your neighbors, ex-coworkers, ex-clients, classmates, associates, family, extended family, and members of special interest groups (church, associations)—and remember that some people may be in more than one category. This exercise will show you where your strengths are, and it will show you who is missing from your network (or your life).

2. *Stay in contact.* Stay in contact with your network. Don't contact people only when you need something; instead, contact them occasionally just to say hello or to offer your assistance to others. When you do ask for

something, be specific. Make it easy for others to help you.

A mistake made by many people who are in a career transition is to send an email to everyone in their database saying, "I still need a job; send me all leads." What, exactly, is the reader supposed to do?

A better approach is to send an email to an appropriate group within your network saying, "I've targeted a few companies I'd like to learn more about; if you have any contacts with these organizations, I'd love to talk with you about an introduction. I will not be asking you—or them—for a job; I'm at the information-gathering stage."

A word about badgering:

There are reasons why people within your network and outside of your network will not talk to you:

1. They do not know you.
2. They are too busy.
3. They are afraid that you will pressure them for a job.

Then there are the reasons why they will talk to you:

1. They know you personally.
2. They know the person referring you to be credible.
3. You let them know what your intentions are concerning this meeting.

Any networking plan has to take into account the fact that the currently employed are bombarded with requests for their time. Some networkers pull a "bait and switch" on their target, initially declaring that they are simply gathering information, and then pouncing with résumé in hand as soon as the office door opens. This approach ruins not only your credibility but the credibility of the person who referred you. Being eager to land a great job is a good thing; being desperate is not.

Targeting   No networking plan is complete or likely to be successful without targeting. Targeting is the process of identifying where you want to work, from a geographic and an industry perspective. You then build your network around your targets. To start, ask yourself:

- What geographic territories are options for me?

- What industries exist within those territories that would value my skills?

- What companies within those industries would hire someone like me?

- Which of those companies do I admire enough to work for?

- Whom do I know, or whom do I need to know, within my target companies?

Targeting and networking go together. To make them work well, you need to develop relationships, research companies, and conduct networking meetings in an effort to generate offers.

Networking Meetings   Through your targeting and networking efforts, you will get introductions to contacts at the targeted companies you have selected. The next step is to ask for a meeting or interview with each of those contacts. In this meeting, you are interviewing the contact, not the other way around. You will let the target contact know that your purpose for the meeting you are requesting is to gather information on industry trends, on the company and its initiatives, on the person you are speaking with—even on the corporate and division goals for the next quarter (or year). Make it clear in your request that you will not be asking for a job—and keep this commitment.

To conduct a meaningful networking meeting, you will need to have done your homework on the industry, the company, its competitors, and any recent news. Use the library, the Internet, and your network of contacts. Prepare for your networking meeting by creating a list of questions to ask that show that you are interested, and that will guide you in your decision as to whether this company is a place where you would really like to work. Ask questions in each of the following categories that show your knowledge and interest:

- The industry: "What are the most important trends in this industry right now?"

- The company: "What important challenges is your organization facing right now?"

- The person with whom you are meeting: "What is some advice you would give to someone in my position?"

Create a list of questions that will fit within the allotted time, and remember, a networking meeting is not an excuse to ask for a job. Use this time to gather information; you can always follow up with a job inquiry later.

When you have completed your questioning, alter your exit statement depending on how much you liked or disliked what you learned during the meeting:

1. If you liked what you saw and heard, you might carefully ask, "How do you think someone like me might fit in here at XYZ?" If the answer is negative, then ask, "Who else in the industry do you recommend that I speak with for additional information?"

2. If you did not like what you saw or heard, say, "I'm interested in continuing my research—whom else do you think I should speak with for additional information?"

Managing Your Job Search

Managing an effective job search campaign takes hard work; a substantial amount of time, energy, and determination; and blatant optimism. This process is meant to get you interviews and offers so that you can choose the job you want, not take the job you need.

The first real key to any job search campaign is to call on your best project management skills. Your campaign to find a job is a project like every other project you have managed in your work (and your life). You will use your strategic thinking, preparation, planning, and organizational skills, along with a little common sense.

Your ability to implement your plan with determination and tenacity is even more important given the fact of unreturned phone calls, limited response to direct mail campaigns, and repeated rejections. Rejection (or nonresponse) is a part of this project work. It does not mean that *you* are rejected, it means that for one reason or another, the job does not seem to be a good fit. That reality is certainly more difficult to accept when *you* are not the one making the determination, but it is part of the process that you will manage.

Interviews and Offers

The goal of any job search campaign is to get interviews and offers. If you are not getting interviews, you need to review your up-front work (values, skills, talents, and targets). If you are getting interviews, but no offers, something is missing during the interview process.

In this project to get interviews and offers, you will work out the who-what-how of your career transition: You will define your skill set, your values, your marketing plan, and your target companies, and you will certainly pursue those targets with intelligence and integrity.

The Who   Review Chapter 1 and your Values Worksheet (Exhibit 1-3). Use these results, along with your skills, to develop your professional objective. What do you enjoy in your career, and what would you like to avoid repeating (Exhibit 10-1)? Next, create a vision statement for yourself (Exhibit 6-2), including the most likely titles for your next position. (You will be able to use the results of this work to communicate your value in your résumé and when interviewing, and to evaluate the best cultural fit for your style in the organizations you target).

The What   Next, identify what it is that you want. List at least six potential job titles that would fit you, determine how you will package the services you have to offer (create a résumé), and decide what market segments are most likely to buy those services. Consider the following issues:

- How will you describe yourself in order to establish your credibility?

- What accomplishments best speak to your abilities?

- How can you differentiate yourself from others in the marketplace?

- What potential liabilities do you have (for example, you were terminated or you appear to have been job-hopping), and what strategies can you develop to overcome these potential liabilities?

The How   Next, you will be targeting your market, not looking for jobs that are posted, but looking for those unpublished jobs. You will be selecting the most appropriate geographic areas, the most appropriate industries within those areas, the most appropriate companies within those industries, and the individuals within those companies that you would like to meet, as well as preparing networking strategies to connect with people you know who know the people whom you *want* to know. Each of these phases requires a good deal of research and analysis, planning and organization, and how well you perform each of these phases is a measurement of your job search productivity.

To keep you going in your search, keep track of your contacts on a daily and weekly basis. Using the Job Search Productivity Worksheet (Exhibit 14-1), keep track of the number of hours or minutes you spent on each activity, including research, networking, and interviewing.

At the end of each day, calculate the amount of time you spent on each activity. Your productivity at this point is calcu-

Exhibit 14-1
Job Search Productivity Worksheet

Item	Number of Hours												
Company research													
Networking/phone, email, or letter													
Networking/in person													
Responding to posted positions (Internet/print)													
Researching search firms													
Responding to search firm postings													
Contact with target company													
Interview with hiring manager													
Follow-up and thank-you calls and letters													
Other													
Total Contacts													

lated on the actions you have taken: If you have made significant contacts, if you have conducted significant research, if you have spent time in any of the major categories, you have been productive.

At the end of each week, tally your totals in each area, and review your statistics. Tabulating these daily and weekly successes is important in your assessment of your effectiveness; it is a way to focus your time on the technique with the highest ROI and to gauge your productivity based on your activities. If you are working your plan, but you are not getting interviews, you can easily see what part of your campaign you need to change. If you are getting interviews, but no offers, you can again see what part of your campaign you need to change.

At the end of each month, ask yourself:

- How many interviews have I had? What generated the interviews (networking, letter writing, recruiters, direct mail, or job postings)?

- How many offers have I had? From what source (networking, letter writing, recruiters, direct mail, or job postings)? If I turned them down, why?

- Which parts of my marketing plan are working well, and which parts of my plan need to be modified?

- How conscientious have I been in following my plan? Where am I least effective, and why? Where am I most effective, and why?

Final Thoughts on Your Road to a New Career

Whether you have been at your job search for 2 weeks or 2 years, making a career transition is a project that requires all of your talent, concentration, determination, and *celebration*. You may be using skills that you have not used in years—shameless self-promotion, blatant optimism, and profound courage.

A career transition can be a slow spiral into self-doubt, or it can be another path to creating a great life for yourself. Develop the support structures you need to help you through it:

- Set strong boundaries for your friends and relatives so that they know how to help you. They may believe they are being helpful when they ask, "Have you found anything yet?" but a better way for them to connect with you would be to ask, "How can I help you with your job search today?"

- Watch yourself talk. If you find yourself in a negative mental process, stop and reframe. Envision the way you want your situation to turn out, and do what you can to make that happen.

- Work with a network friend or a coach to define your own who-what-how plan.

- Acknowledge the productivity milestones that are the hallmarks of success. Keep track of your activities and celebrate your *actions*.

- Create and maintain a strong network. Nourishing the relationships you develop during this process of career transition will not only increase your circle of friends but also keep you in touch with the unpublished job market in the years to come.

Concepts to Remember

1. Know and master the four routes to your new career.

2. Spend your job search time on those methods that are most likely to provide the highest ROI.

3. Understand the difference between retained and contingent recruiters, and understand what they can do for you.

4. Learn to network well.

5. Target the companies you would like to work for, even if they don't have any published job openings.

6. Develop a good elevator speech.

7. When networking in a group or individually, be sure to clearly state what it is that you want.

8. Stay in contact with your network, and offer to assist the people in it whenever you can.

9. Know why people in your network *will not* talk to you, and change your approach so that they will.

10. Use the networking meeting as a process for expanding your network and tapping into the unpublished job market.

11. Manage your job search campaign like a project, and keep track of what is working.

12. Develop your career "who-what-how" process, and create your plan to get a job you love.

PART 4

CAREER CONTROL

Just before I decided to take control of my own career, I was suffering from corporate misery. I did not realize just how unhappy I was until I removed myself from the clutter and confusion of my corporate life and began to take a closer look.

In my corporate career, I have worked for bosses who did not like me and for bosses that I disliked; I have had coworkers who were downright mean and coworkers who were supportive and kind. I have played office politics and lost, and I have played office politics and "won" but still lost. I have been promoted, laid off, and fired.

It was not until I discovered who I was in terms of values, strengths, skills, boundaries, and needs that I was able to move ahead in my career and my life. And it was only *then* that I uncovered what I wanted for myself, and only then that I could set a plan to go get it.

In coaching my clients, I have found that many of them have had similar experiences, and through the processes in this book, they have each made choices that enabled them to escape that corporate misery and create successful and fulfilled lives, with careers that honor who they are and what they do best.

Having a job you love as part of a life you love is available to you—all you need to do is take action. Part of the action you take will be to *choose* to change, while also choosing to be happy in your pursuit of happiness.

Everyone deserves a career that brings out his or her best. Decide to make that happen for yourself by first identifying the gap between where you are right now and where you want to be. Commit to learning more about who you are and what you want, then take control of your career and get it.

15

Taking Control

Consider this: Since we are all living longer than people in generations past, if we start our professional careers in our early twenties, we will be in the workforce for a period of 45 to 50 years. Now, if you hate your job, working for 50 years sounds like a horrifying proposition. If you love your job, however, working for 50 years sounds more like a gift. If you love what you do, you will want to keep doing it, because it uses your strengths and talents, continually enhances your skills, honors your values, and allows you to be professionally successful and personally fulfilled at the same time.

Take control of your career, and you will be taking control of your life.

Resources

The following organizations and web sites are offered as resources
for additional information:

- Coaching, assessments, and workshops: Executive
  Coaching and Resource Network: www.Executive-
  Coaching.com

- In-person executive networking opportunities:
  Executive-Networking (west coast): www.executive-
  networking.com
  ExecuNet (nationwide): www.execunet.com
  C-Sixgroups:.yahoo.com/group/csixnetwork
  FortyPlus of Bay Area: www.fortyplus.org/
  Financial Executives Networking Group: www.thefeng.
  org/home.html
  Marketing Executives Networking Group: www.men
  gonline.com/

- For a national database of networking groups: www.
  careerjournal.com/calendar/index.html

- Virtual executive networking opportunities:
  Ryze www.ryze.com

- Nationwide expert career management resources for
  executives and professionals: www.ExecuNet.com

- Legal advice for employees: Executive Law Group, www.
  execlaw.com

- Coach referral services, some with a sliding scale and pro bono coaching:
  International Coach Federation: www.coachfederation. org
  Coachville: www.coachvillereferral.com
  Coach Inc.: www.coachinc.com

- For healing:
  Therapist Referral Network: www.therapy-referral.com
  Therapist Directory: www.psychology.com/therapist/

- Directory of recruiters and other search resources:
  www.i-recruit.com
  www.searchfirm.com/
  www.executive-coaching.com/searchresources.htm

- Better Business Bureau: www.bbb.com

Index

About the Author

Linda Dominguez is the founder and principal of Executive Coaching and Resource Network and has worked with more than 500 executives and leaders to advance their careers. She is also a regular contributor to the *Wall Street Journal, Fortune,* and other business and career publications.